A Man in All Seasons
Volume 2

A Handbook for
Faithful Living

Volume 2

A Man in All

Seasons

Edited by
Thomas A. Jones

DPI
DISCIPLESHIP
PUBLICATIONS
INTERNATIONAL

A Man in All Seasons — Volume 2
© 2001 by Discipleship Publications International
2 Sterling Road, Billerica, Mass. 01862-2595

Printed in the United States of America

ISBN: 1-57782-166-1

Cover Design: Christine Nolan
Interior Design: Corey Fisher

To Bernie Alspaugh,

whose chapter in Volume 1 powerfully reminded

us that nothing can separate us from the

love of God that is in Christ Jesus our Lord

Contents

Sexuality, Marriage & Family

Special Challenges

Introduction

I want men everywhere to lift up holy hands in prayer,
without anger or disputing.

1 Timothy 2:8

Men in our generation do not enjoy a great reputation. As a man,
I am often embarrassed by my gender. There are the spoiled
athletes making millions of dollars a year, but who complain about
their coaches and seem to have no understanding of team. There are
the politicians who lead two (or more) lives and then expect us to
believe their lies. There are the loud obnoxious types who dominate
talk radio. There are the dads who are not respected by their children
and the husbands whose wives long for some emotional connection
with them. Quite contrary to God's plan, the main emotion that men
are known for is anger. The most lucrative Internet business of all is
the pornography industry, which is, of course, almost completely
fueled by males who give in to "a continual lust for more"
(Ephesians 4:19).

There are few heroes. Most people strain to name even one. I
read this week about a group of several hundred "lost boys" that
were brought to the United States from a Third World country to
begin a new life. I was struck by the thought that many men—
though they are in the First World and are trained and educated—
are still "lost boys," never having gone on to the emotional,
relational and spiritual maturity that God intended.

In this series of handbooks for men, our goal is to shine the
light of the gospel of Jesus on issues that men face, so that we might
find help to become the spiritual men, leaders, protectors—and
yes—even heroes, that God made us to be.

Many of us who have been disciples for a number of years have
found that our level of conviction and determination must grow as
we journey on. The faith we had and the victories we won yesterday
will not suffice for the new challenges we face today. Our reliance on

God and his grace must continually increase. Our goal with these books is to call us back to ever-crucial fundamentals and to tackle new issues that test our faith and resolve.

The truth is that from Adam onward, men have often not distinguished themselves. However, whenever men have humbled themselves and recognized their need for God, they have become men that have made a difference in the lives of others. Whatever our circumstances, whatever our challenges, God will be faithful to us, and we can be used powerfully by him. It is our prayer that this book will help thousands of men to that end.

Thomas Jones
September 2001

Additional note: As we were entering the last stages of our work on this book prior to sending it to the printer, the tragic events in the Northeast shocked the nation and the world. On the desk in front of me is the latest issue of Time *magazine. The only words on the cover are "September 11, 2001." That day will forever be etched in our memories. The events of the day remind us that there has never been a greater need for men of God with deep convictions who handle their challenges with integrity and faith. Our prayer continues to be that this series of books will help men everywhere to rise up and be a light in the midst of darkness.*

Walk with God

1

Spirituality

Sam Laing

The spiritual man makes judgments about all things, but he himself is not subject to any man's judgment:

> "For who has known the mind of the Lord
>   that he may instruct him?"

But we have the mind of Christ.

1 Corinthians 2:15-16

One cannot be a mighty man of God without being a spiritual man. It is spirituality that gives us our power. Spirituality is the mysterious quality that imparts to our lives a unique dimension that sets us apart. Being a spiritual man is about depending on the power of God. If we reach for the stars but rely on ourselves, we will fall back to earth exhausted, defeated and discouraged. It is spirituality that will take us to the heights, that will enable us to radically and permanently change.

A man can be no mightier than his relationship with God allows. If then we want to be mighty men of God, we must seek to know God, to love him and to be his friends. We cannot come to God for power, strength and transformation and neglect being close to him. He does not give his gifts for our own use or on our terms, but for his glory and in his way.

Depth

Many of us are focused on *doing,* not on *being.* We want to work, accomplish and achieve for God, but we do not desire to draw near to God and deal with our inner selves. Venturing into the deep waters frightens us, so we wade in the shallows. We do not think deeply, feel deeply or love deeply. We are lightweights. Others sense that we are just actors, putting on a show. We lack depth, and it shows in every aspect of our lives.

We cannot talk to our wives because we are shallow. We lack influence with our children because we are shallow. We lack deep friendships because we are shallow. We cannot express ourselves, and have little to say when we do, because we are shallow. When we have much to say, our words fall to the ground anyway, because we are shallow. We do not change, or do not change for long, because we are shallow. We are lonely, depressed, discouraged and empty because we are shallow. We are weak men, not mighty men, because *we are shallow!*

But God did not make us shallow. He made us with hearts that can feel, think and be. He made us like himself. We have minds, souls and spirits. We are more than machines—we are *men.* The problem is not that we are fundamentally flawed; the problem is that we will not deepen ourselves. We will not let ourselves go beyond the surface. We prefer to keep things on a superficial level because we fear what we, or others, might find if we went deeper. We seek to avoid pain and instead choose a lifetime of aching emptiness. We seek to avoid embarrassment and instead find the isolation that pride brings. We seek to protect ourselves with shallowness but it becomes the instrument of our destruction.

God works from the inside out. God looks at who you really are, not what you appear to be. As he selected the next king to lead his people, he told the prophet Samuel,

> "Do not consider his appearance or his height, for I have rejected him. The LORD does not look at the things man looks at. Man looks at the outward appearance, but the LORD looks at the heart." (1 Samuel 16:7)

David, the leader of the mighty men, was preeminently a man of heart, of spirituality. David was a man who loved God in a deeply personal way. He prayed. He sang songs of worship; he poured out his heart. The psalms he wrote continue to live on thousands of years later because they speak of a relationship with God that we all long for. David's spirituality was the secret of his almost magical power of leadership. His men were fiercely loyal to him and gave him their complete trust because they knew he was a spiritual man, a man who walked with God.

Consistent Study

First, a spiritual man is a man of God's word. We must become men who take God's word into our deepest selves. The Bible is a double-edged sword that is meant to penetrate to the depths of our souls. Yet for many of us, those feelings are but a distant memory from the days of our conversion. We now have hard, tired, dull hearts that have lost the sense of awe of God's love and holiness. How can we get our hearts tender again? It will take effort, the effort of intense, regular, personal Bible study. It will mean getting out our Bibles and begging God to speak to us from them once again. It will mean taking notes, agonizing over passages and letting them apply to our lives as we did in the past. It will mean spending more than a few minutes a day studying—it will mean carving out more time in our schedules and devoting some late nights, early mornings, half-days and whole days to digging into the Word.

It will mean committing God's word to memory. One of the challenges I gave our Mighty Man group in Triangle was to commit chapters and sections of the Bible to memory. My sons memorized the entire book of 2 Timothy. As they recited it before one of our meetings, the men present were moved to tears. What an incredible effort, and what an incredible reward all of us reaped from it!

Devoted Prayer

A spiritual man is devoted to prayer (Colossians 4:2). This will mean getting up early like Jesus did so that you can pray undisturbed before you start your day. It will involve going to a quiet place to pray, where you are completely alone and can pour out your soul to God. It may entail going to the private room that Jesus talked about (Matthew 6:6) or someplace outdoors. It will mean taking some time to get away by yourself, all alone, so that you can pray more fervently. It will mean learning to pray out loud. It will call for praying on your knees and with your hands raised to heaven. It will include praying with a loud voice and with tears. It will require learning to pray constantly, bringing God into the details of your everyday life. It will take everything we have got and more! But the rewards of being a spiritual man are too great—we cannot back away from the challenge!

Most of us bear more sorrow, more anxiety and burdens than we know. We worry about our families, our finances and our futures. We go through life nagged constantly by unsettling anxiety. We need to learn to cast all of our burdens, from the most weighty to the most mundane, upon our loving Father in heaven. We cannot do this in an off-handed, cursory manner. It is going to take real effort. For most of us, this will mean that the amount and quality of personal time with God that we have been spending is going to have to significantly increase.

Continual Growth

Some of us are at the same place in our relationship with God where we were years ago. No wonder we are shallow! We are still living at the level of a spiritual infant. We are still worldly and unspiritual because we have not progressed beyond our early days as Christians. Our prayer lives, Bible study and depth of communion with God are static, yet our lives have only become more complicated and challenging as time has gone by. We read the same verses, spend the same amount of time and follow the same spiritual routine day in and day out. Some of us may even desire to be closer to God but are too lazy to put in the effort. It is our laziness that is stunting our spiritual growth and leaving us sadly deficient in spirituality. We must go further, take more time and take it deeper than we ever have before if we are to become mighty men of God.

Men, we are talking about a *relationship* here. Your friendship with God is either getting deeper, or it is dying. It cannot be set up, then put on hold or in a cruise-control mode. Imagine taking that same attitude with your wife. Imagine being married for years, but never coming to know each other any better, never getting closer. What an empty shell of a marriage that would be! Yet that is just what many of us men have done with God. We think, *Okay, I'm saved, so I have my relationship with God covered. Now let me go on and do something else.* It just doesn't work that way! Relationships need to grow, and to grow they must be nurtured.

Begin today. Decide that you are going to seek to know God, to draw nearer to him than ever before. Repent of your unspiritual, superficial devotion. Then decide that you will spend some extra time with God. I would urge you as soon as possible to take at least one night and day and get away completely by yourself. Fast if you need to. Do as the mighty men of the Bible did—spend time alone with God, in large quantities, as often as you need to. Develop consistency in your daily devotions. Learn to pour your heart out in prayer, and open your heart to God's word. Decide that your relationship with God will begin anew and that you will never again allow it to become stagnant or dull. Decide that every day you will fight to grow closer to God, no matter what the cost—and watch as you experience a spiritual glory and joy that David wrote about:

> O God, you are my God,
>> earnestly I seek you;
> my soul thirsts for you,
>> my body longs for you,
> in a dry and weary land
>> where there is no water.
> I have seen you in the sanctuary
>> and beheld your power and your glory.
> Because your love is better than life,
>> my lips will glorify you.
> I will praise you as long as I live,
>> and in your name I will lift up my hands.
> My soul will be satisfied as with the richest of foods;
>> with singing lips my mouth will praise you. (Psalm 63:1-5)

This chapter was reprinted from *Mighty Man of God* © 1999 Discipleship Publications International and is available through the DPI Web site at www.dpibooks.org.

2

Living with Passion
Mike Fontenot

Throughout history, words often change their meaning. For example, "hostile" in the English language morphed into "host" as people began to realize that it was better for survival to treat strangers kindly—"hospitable" is a related word—rather than to kill them instantly as a threat. And many other examples abound. One such change is with the word "passion." In the English language of our day, "passion" more often than not connotes sensuality. But historically when people thought of passion, they often thought of Christ. "Passion plays" were dramatizations of the crucifixion of Jesus. The "passion fruit" was named because its flower has a cross protruding from the interior of the flower—not because of some south-seas-island, exotic sensuality.

Jesus' Passion
So, what is Biblical passion all about? Let's take a look at Jesus' life. In John 2 he attended a wedding at Cana "on the third day." Weddings were held on the third day because this was the first day that God said "It was good" twice (Genesis 1:9-13). Considered a twice-blessed day, it is still the most popular wedding day in Israel today. During this wedding, a social calamity arose, and Jesus' mother informed him, "They have no more wine" (John 2:3). Weddings in the first century lasted as long as the refreshments. So, this wedding was going to have a premature, disgraceful end. After

Jesus changed a great quantity of water to wine, the wedding coordinator was shocked, remarking to the bridegroom, of all people, that normally the best is first, then later, the cheaper wine comes out once the palates have been dulled. This was Jesus' first miracle, saving the day for the wedding party.

Jesus then entered the temple. There he found a spiritual party that also had been going on for a long time that had also symbolically run out of wine. The guests' ability, as well, to discern quality had disappeared, in the same way that the wedding guests' palates had lost their ability to discern the quality of the wine as the party progressed. In the temple, gone were the days of Solomon's glorious dedication with splendor and awe (they didn't even last his lifetime), the days of Zerubbabel and Ezra, even the days of Herod. Jesus walked into the temple area and found plenty of religion. There were horns, animals, processions and drama. It was all form, but no quality; all functional correctness, but spiritual deadness; all outward magnificence, but inward dullness! So, Jesus made a whip and drove out the livestock and overturned the money-changers' tables. This reminded the disciples of the Old Testament passage: "Zeal for your house will consume me" (Psalm 6:9, quoted in John 2:17).

"Zeal" and "passion" are related words, Biblically. As godly men, what should "passion" mean for us? Let's consider three areas of passion that we need.

Unlike the World's

First, Biblical passion needs to be a passion unlike the world's. "Passion," as has been said, is usually used in a sinful way in our world, often with sinful connotations. In Hosea 7:4-7 it says:

> They are all adulterers,
>> burning like an oven
> whose fire the baker need not stir
>> from the kneading of the dough till it rises.
> On the day of the festival of our king
>> the princes become inflamed with wine,
>> and he joins hands with the mockers.
> Their hearts are like an oven;
>> they approach him with intrigue.

> Their passion smolders all night;
>> in the morning it blazes like a flaming fire.
> All of them are hot as an oven;
>> they devour their rulers.
> All their kings fall,
>> and none of them calls on me.

This is a good definition of worldly passion, a passion described as an oven in our hearts, burning in the night. The apostle Paul talks of having pure relationships with the opposite sex, "not in passionate lust like the heathen who do not know God" (1 Thessalonians 4:5). The Greek word here, *epitemee,* which is translated as "lust or worldly passion" is also used in Titus 2:12 in which the grace of God teaches us to say no to such worldly passions. Titus 3:3 repeats the same worldly emphasis describing our previous non-Christian days as being "foolish, disobedient, deceived and enslaved by all kinds of *passions* and pleasures" (emphasis added).

All of these verses remind godly men that we are not to be controlled by burning passions which focus on sexuality, materialism and hedonistic living (loving pleasure). That you are reading this chapter most likely means that you have made a decision to be a disciple and to not be like the world—not driven by the same passions. We are totally unlike the world!

Another kind of heart is described vividly in Jeremiah 20:9:

> But if I say, "I will not mention him
>> or speak any more in his name,"
> his word is in my heart like a fire,
>> a fire shut up in my bones.
> I am weary of holding it in;
>> indeed, I cannot.

There is a fire in our hearts that burns so brightly that even if we try to restrain it or calm ourselves down, it spills out. The very effort required to *not* talk about our God and the gospel needs to exhaust us! I pray you can understand, can relate to, and can be so inspired that you are pained when you are restricted by your employer or other circumstances from opening your mouth.

Marked by Sacrifice

Second, not only is our passion to be unlike the worlds' but it must be marked by sacrifice. Pure Biblical passion is historically about sacrifice. The Late Latin word for suffering is *passio*, from which we get the English word "passion." In Greek, suffering is *pascho*, from which comes "the paschal lamb," "the sacrificed lamb." Passion as suffering has all but disappeared in the English language. But a Passion play, as I mentioned before, is specifically about the suffering and sacrifice of Jesus. And the power of passion is seen in the willingness of one to sacrifice and to suffer.

There is a sharp contrast between the passion of the world, which is all about self-living and self-gratification, and the passion of Christ, which is all about selfless living. As men, we are drawn to great acts of sacrifice. It is hard not to be moved by Tom Brokaw's moving stories of what he calls "the greatest generation," those men and women of World War II days who did their duty for their country and families. If our generation in God's kingdom is to be remembered as great, then the same stories of selfless service to our spiritual kingdom need to be lived out in our lives. As Jesus has said, if we would be great, then we must be servants of all. Not only do we need to understand our role as servants, but we need to embrace this role with great passion. It needs to burn in our hearts and set us on fire. Are we zealously eager to serve, or is it all a tired, old burden? Do we begrudgingly serve, or is it a fire that burns within? Is the wine of service running out in our lives?

> There is a sharp contrast between the passion of the world, which is all about self-living and self-gratification, and the passion of Christ, which is all about selfless living.

Just Like Jesus'

Third and last, we must have a passion like our Lord Jesus. John 2:1-17 recounts back-to-back incidents in the early days of Jesus' ministry. He changed water to wine and then proceeded to go to Jerusalem to dramatically cleanse the temple. After these events, John records one brief sentence: "His disciples remembered that it is written: 'Zeal for your house will consume me'" (John 2:17). They recalled a quote from Psalm 69:8-9:

> I am a stranger to my brothers,
>> an alien to my own mother's sons;
> for zeal for your house consumes me,
>> and the insults of those who insult you fall on me.

In John 7:5 it says that "even his own brothers did not believe in him." I'm sure that it wasn't just his beliefs that put his brothers off, but his zeal for those beliefs. His family came to take him away (Mark 3:20-21), not for some doctrinal issue about Messianic fulfillment, but because he wasn't eating properly. In my own experience, it wasn't my doctrinal beliefs that upset my family and created tension. It was my zeal for my faith that caused the concern! I can still see the concerned stare of my mother, not at all about doctrinal truths, but about the passion I expressed when talking about my God. How about you? Have we lost so much of our passion that our families are no longer even bothered by our lifestyle?

What is zeal? "Zeal" and "jealousy" are from the same word, Biblically. Even in English you can see the similarity. Cain and Abel, Joseph and his brothers, and Saul and David all had a jealousy that led to acts of violence. The two greatest examples of zeal in the Old Testament are Phinehas and Jehu. Phinehas becomes the model of godly, passionate zeal when he sees a Hebrew taking a Moabite woman to bed and impales them both in the act of immorality (Numbers 25:1ff). His zeal, expressed in his violent action, stopped the plague that God had sent:

> "Phinehas son of Eleazar, the son of Aaron, the priest, has turned my anger away from the Israelites; for he was as zealous as I am for my honor among them, so that in my zeal I did not put an end to them. Therefore tell him I am making my covenant of peace with him. He and his descendants will have a covenant of a lasting priesthood, because he was zealous for the honor of his God and made atonement for the Israelites."

Jehu, in the same way, in his zeal and passion, was God's instrument of justice on the house of Omri (Ahab). His violent passion and zeal in purifying Israel from the likes of Jezebel and company sets a Biblical standard that has inspired disciples over the years: "Jehu said, 'Come with me and see my *zeal* for the LORD'" (2 Kings 10:16, emphasis added).

In John 2, the one scripture that mentions Jesus' zeal in the New Testament, is also associated with the somewhat violent act of driving out of the temple those who were defiling its premises. Now Jesus' violence is not at all like the violence of the Old Testament. His behavior is much more like a parent disciplining his child. Under the new covenant, we must never express our zeal for God with acts of violence as a Christian. But true passion and zeal are so deep that there is an air of radicalness about them. Be careful. Don't confuse this with hype. Zeal here is not about, "Let's get fired up, let's get louder, let's be happy!" All of that can be great, but Biblical zeal is about great heartfelt passion for God and his causes and purposes in our world. Your goal should never be to alienate anyone, but do you have enough passion to alienate anyone? Jesus had a zeal so radical that it disturbed others. How is yours?

An Undiluted Passion

Jesus, while clearing out the temple, said, "'Get these out of here! How dare you turn my Father's house into a market!'" (John 2:16). The Greek word for "market" is *emporion*, from which we get the English word "emporium," a place of trade. These agents of the emporium, who were like wholesalers, were called *kapeleuo* or "peddlers." Paul uses the same word in 2 Corinthians 2:17:

> Unlike so many, we do not peddle the word of God for profit. On the contrary, in Christ we speak before God with sincerity, like men sent from God.

The most famous and common kind of peddlers were the wine traders. The very word carried the nuances of trickery and greed because they would water down their wine and sell it as the unadulterated product (a practice that still occasionally makes the news). So, when Paul said he was not a peddler of the word of God, he used the metaphor of not being one who watered down the message for personal gain. Jesus, the abundant supplier of the best wine, expects us to never, ever—never—water down the message of the gospel to make it more palatable to the majority of people. He does not want us to mislead a lost world by reducing the quality of discipleship to a mere semblance of the genuine lifestyle. Like the metaphor of salt that has lost its taste, so this wine looks like wine, tastes a bit like wine, but it has lost its punch and vitality, having been corrupted by those seeking quick growth at the expense of heartfelt dedication.

These are our greatest temptations and our greatest dangers: "Let's compromise what it means to be a Christian or how to become one." "Let's compromise what the life of a disciple is meant to be!" "Let's compromise the depth of our commitment and the depth of our sacrifice!"

As the party at the wedding went on and on, the ability to discern, to know what was best was lost with time, familiarity and exposure (John 2:10). In Jesus' day in the temple, gone were the glorious days of Solomon dedicating the temple—they were gone before they buried him. Gone were the days of Ezra and Zerubbabel dedicating the restored temple, days of sacrifice and commitment. All that was left in Jesus' day was form and habit, but no passion.

An Unending Passion

Well, brothers, the party in our day has been going on and on. Some of you have been Christians for a long time now. How is your passion holding out? When we have a missions contribution, do you still have the same passion about seeing the world evangelized? Or does it just seem like paying your dues for the club? Do you still have passion about your personal outreach? Do you still have passion about having close, open relationships in God's community? Are you passionately seeking a great relationship with Jesus? The only solution is to keep drinking of the wine that Jesus abundantly supplies. The oversupply at the wedding simply illustrates that his resources are lavishly available. The great news of Jesus' miracle is that the best wine is always waiting to be had—the best is yet to be. This is not just about the new covenant and heaven, but also about growing old in the kingdom of God: Our best years are yet to be!

How passionate are you about this? This is the zeal that disturbs. This is the passion that separates, and yet the passion that brings together those who are looking for life. In the movie, *Ever After*, a remake of the Cinderella tale, there is one scene in which the prince, who is jaded about having all and having nothing, is drawn to this girl (Cinderella character) who amazes him at how passionately she feels about issues and justice and integrity. His life, being so shallow, is drawn to her zest for life. Our passion, as well, most certainly draws in those jaded by the world, who go shopping at the marketplaces of life and are sick of all the junk available to them, who are looking for real valuables in life: meaning and purpose. As God's men, we need to be recognized by our passion. Would Jesus notice you?

3

First...the Kingdom
Randy McKean

"But seek first his kingdom and his righteousness, and all these things will be given to you as well."

Matthew 6:33

Jesus' great sermon reaches a crescendo. First...the kingdom! Now *everything* changes. Everything must be reexamined. Everything must be rescrutinized. Everything must be reconsidered. *Everything*! Every dream, every plan, every desire, every use of money, every use of time—everything must have a kingdom-first focus. It's no longer what self wants, now it's what God wants. It's no longer what builds me up the most, it's what builds God's kingdom and God's people up the most. It's no longer "Where can I be most comfortable?" Now it's "Where can I be most effective?" Now, it's "How can I be most used?" not "How can I be most happy?"

New Dreams

Before becoming a disciple, my goal was to become a successful lawyer. I dreamed of financial wealth and security. I planned to own a prestigious home and to drive only the best of cars. I wanted to have a mountain retreat for weekend getaways. I dreamed of writing books and living in warm climates. I was a relatively moral, nonconfrontive, quiet kind of person. One of my greatest fears in life was public speaking because I was consumed with wondering what others were thinking about me. I was the typical "seek first myself" and "seek first the world" kind of guy. But becoming a disciple radically changed my whole approach toward life. I had to replan and redream my life so that it had a kingdom-first emphasis and focus.

I don't believe that every disciple will change professions or that every disciple will sell all his possessions or that every disciple will move far away from his home and family. I do believe every disciple must seriously consider these possibilities and must be absolutely willing to do these. Certainly, a true kingdom-first attitude always brings radical results. Everything is to become prioritized in relationship to the kingdom immediately—our education, our professions, our family, our relationships and our recreation. At baptism the process begins—the kingdom-first perspective that will forever shape our lives must no longer be theory but practice. Our lives are to be consumed by the kingdom. The kingdom is to be our passion more and more. The kingdom is to be our love more and more. The kingdom is to be our life. Question: How can everything you previously planned, dreamed and desired automatically become God's will for your life? Question: How can your pre-kingdom plans automatically be kingdom-first plans when you never considered the kingdom before? Obviously they can't be! Then how can a person's life be so much the same in goals, passions, desires and dreams? Obviously, again, they can't be. It all has to do with having, or not having, a "First…the Kingdom" heart.

How to Tell

How can you tell when you are *not* seeking first the kingdom?

1. When you don't have daily time with God in prayer and Bible study.

2. When your basic responsibilities to the church are a struggle and not a joy.

3. When special church events (retreats, devotionals, workshops, etc.) feel like a burden instead of an opportunity and a privilege.

4. When you are not happy or not consistent in giving what you promised to God either in weekly contribution or in special missions contributions.

5. When you don't automatically give more when you are blessed with more.

6. When the greatest issues that help determine your life decisions are personal comfort, personal desires, family concerns, money offers or worldly prestige.

7. When you can't find the time to effectively share your faith and study the Bible with people.

8. When you gain greater feelings of accomplishment and satisfaction serving the financial kingdom, the educational kingdom, or the professional kingdom as opposed to God's spiritual kingdom.

9. When you have a greater regard and protection concerning your personal schedule than you have in protecting the kingdom schedule.

10. When discipleship times, family times and devotional times with your spouse and children are not both bonding and spiritually challenging times shared consistently together.

11. When your talents and gifts get used in the world while only the leftovers go into the kingdom.

12. When there is a greater demonstration of your leadership capabilities in the world than in the kingdom.

13. When gaining one more thing is of greater value than gaining one more soul.

14. When your dreams center more in this world than in the kingdom.

15. When you feel greater excitement, happiness, challenge and thrill in the world than in the kingdom of God.

Honestly, are you seeking first the kingdom? Is your life consumed by the kingdom and sold out for the kingdom? The kingdom life is filled with worship services, special spiritual enrichment programs and activities, long and loving fellowships, discipling times, winning as many as possible, serving brothers and sisters in Christ, helping the poor and needy, personal Bible study and prayer. But this is not simply a life of appointments and responsibilities—it is a purposeful, joyful lifestyle designed to aggressively spread the kingdom of God around the world. The kingdom consists of people who are volunteer soldiers in a battle between good and evil. The kingdom is an advancing army bent on penetrating every nation for the glory of our God. The kingdom is made of sacrificial warriors persuading, pleading and urging all in their path to follow King Jesus and to unite together in his glorious kingdom. To serve whole-heartedly in this spiritual army must be our commitment, our dream, our goal, our desire, our passion, our pleasure—our life. Deep in our hearts there must always abide an intense desire that daily demands, "First…the Kingdom!"

Originally published in *First…the Kingdom* ©1994 by Discipleship Publications International.

4

Meet Your Enemy
Mike Taliaferro

The lion has roared—
who will not fear?

Amos 3:8

The dark night sky was slowly brightening into a crimson sunrise and light began creeping over a cool eastern horizon. It was going to be another clear South African morning. Somewhere near the Mozambican border, a zebra stood perfectly motionless, peering into the forest. Something seemed strange. The wind was at her back, and she saw nothing unusual. Yet something was not right.

Earlier she had been with the herd as they grazed in the meadow. She felt secure in their number. The grass was good and the air was cool. She hardly noticed that her companions had moved on. Just a bit more to eat, and she would go too. But then she heard something. A small branch cracking, or a funny rustling of the grass. Hardly noticeable to a human, the strange noise was like an alarm siren to the zebra. Fear gripped her as she realized she was being watched. But she did not know which way to run, and who or how many were out there. She was very anxious, and it took all her self-control to remain motionless. She stood like a statue for twenty minutes.

In the tall grass two eyes stared coldly at the zebra. The lioness was hungry yet cautious. It had been several days since she had eaten, but she knew it was not yet time. She peered through the grass, crouching low, tail down, chin near the ground, waiting. On her far left and right were two other lionesses inching unseen toward the zebra; soon they would be in position. Behind the huntresses were the male and the cubs; the 450-pound male had chosen not to hunt that morning.

A few meters away, the zebra faltered. The fear of being alone surpassed the fear of some unknown beast in the grass. She turned slowly and began to move deliberately toward the herd. Ever alert, she unknowingly turned her back to the leading lioness.

Seizing the moment, the lioness moved forward through the grass. Totally camouflaged, she moved quickly with her head and tail low, still in a crouched position.

Then the zebra heard it: a horrifying roar, a loud, terrifying sound that she could actually feel. Its purpose was to intimidate her, and it succeeded. The zebra was spooked and quickly turned her head in fright. She glanced into the grass for a split second before she spotted the charging beast. She turned and ran. But it was too late. Once moving, a lion can cover the length of a basketball court in just over one second.

The first lioness slammed into the zebra at shoulder height, sending both animals tumbling in a cloud of dust and grass. Losing all sense of direction, the panicked zebra struggled to get back on her feet. Streaking through the air came the paw of the second lioness, who had charged close behind the first. As the razor-sharp two-inch-long talons sliced through the zebra's skin and neck muscles, the force of the blow knocked her off balance again. As she fell backward, the first lioness bit down hard on the her neck. With its teeth sinking in deeply, the beast crushed her windpipe as if she were caught in a vise grip. The zebra struggled to move, but the lioness' hold on her neck was unbreakable. She would be unconscious in a moment, but the lions did not wait. Hunger spurred them on as they ripped into the zebra's bowels. Indeed, her last experience of life would be the excruciating pain of being eaten alive. The zebra lay there stunned and dying, the pain of suffocation exceeded only by the agony of her flesh being torn apart. Soon the light faded from her eyes entirely.

Now the entire pride gathered. The male, as well as his three female partners, situated themselves at the key positions for devouring their meal. The little cubs pushed to eat but they would eat only after the adults were full.

In the grass a hundred meters away, some hyenas watched closely. They knew the sun's heat would drive the lions into the shade later in the day. They waited for a chance to steal some choice body parts. Vultures, too, began to hover.

But in this game park another animal soon approached. His vehicle could be heard, seen and smelled as many as two kilometers away. It came, clumsily bounding over the ground, belching forth the queer odor of burning petrol. Voices came from within this metal and glass box. Then the box stopped, only yards away from the kill. The voices inside were hushed. The noise and smell seemed to be over for the most part.

The lions hardly noticed. With faces covered in blood, panting heavily, and with strings of intestine stuck in their teeth, they continued the arduous and frenzied task of ripping the flesh off the zebra's bones. The lions were eating everything. The muscle, fat, gristle, bowels and ligaments were all consumed. If they were hungry enough, they would have even eaten the bones. Sometimes, when a human is eaten, only a heel bone or shoulder blade is left over.

Later one would describe the scene as commonplace. Two men in a Land Rover. Ten lions eating their breakfast. Hyenas and vultures in the distance. A typical African morning.

Grass in Africa can grow up to six feet tall, making photography difficult. In the Land Rover, one man felt his classic photo was being ruined by the tall grass. He thought for a moment. He debated. Then he made a momentous decision. He opened the door of the vehicle and stepped down into the grass. He positioned himself five or six meters (approximately 16-20 feet) from the vehicle, camera in hand. His new position improved his view of the lions greatly. Little did he realize though that he had stepped down from the vehicle and onto the front page of every major South African daily newspaper.

Physically man is no match for the lion. In a 100-meter race, the lion would cross the finish line in under four seconds just as the fastest human reached the thirty meter mark. Only the cheetah is faster. With a running start a lion can jump over a ten meter hole (thirty-nine feet). Deadly accurate, lions have been known to bring down a Cape buffalo with one bite to the spine.

The lion can smell and hear far better than man. His coat makes him almost invisible in the grass. If he so desired, a lion could put two paws against any medium-sized automobile and turn it over. Seemingly the only advantage man has, besides intelligence, is that he sees color where the lion only sees black and white. But how comforting is it to know that you can see him in full color, as 500 pounds of pure carnivore streaks towards you at 115 kph (65 mph)? Three times faster than the fastest human, twice the size of a professional American football player, and practically invisible in his approach, the lion is a terrifying opponent. Even the lion's black-and-white vision becomes an advantage. Diminished color gives them better night vision, which is when they do most of their hunting. They can see in only one-eighth the light that a human needs.

In the game park, the other man watched the lions from the Land Rover. The zebra kill fascinated him. With the camera perched on one knee and his eyes glued to the viewfinder, he stared at the scene. Soon he was clicking the shutter in fascination. He had never seen a kill before. Meanwhile, nearby in the grass, his friend knelt on one knee focusing his lens on the male of the pride whose wet, bloody face kept disappearing into the zebra carcass to rip away more flesh. He would come out for a moment, panting, chewing and swallowing. He seemed oblivious to the two men.

Then it happened. Perhaps a twig snapped. Perhaps the lioness growled. But suddenly the man's attention was riveted to his right. There, crouched low, was the lioness. The same grass which had hidden his view had also hidden her approach.

Staring at the man, the lioness kept her head low and tail against the ground. They stared at each other for a second which seemed like an eternity. His heart was pounding like a bass drum.

Then decidedly he started toward the car. The lioness was in the air in a flash, hitting him full force in the chest. Knocking him down hard, the lioness moved up towards his throat.

Experienced hunters know that once hit, your only hope is to feed the animal your hand and forearm. You can't fend him off completely, but perhaps a friend can fire a shot while the animal takes your wrist.

The man, however, did not think quickly. He only screamed as the jaws closed in on his throat. The lioness clamped down until he lost consciousness. He was dead before any help could arrive.

Inside the vehicle, his friend instinctively clicked the shutter, taking several pictures of the kill. These photos appeared in most of the major dailies in South Africa.

Popular culture warps our image of the lion. We see him in a zoo cage. We see Tarzan killing him in a movie. Our kids cuddle stuffed Simbas from Disney's *Lion King*. He becomes a harmless enigma in our minds. But to stand before the lion, eye to eye without bars, glass or fence, is absolutely horrifying. To hear him breathing, to feel his roar, is simply terrifying. But to be hunted is the sickest feeling of all. In the African savanna, you cannot outrun him, you cannot fight him, and you cannot hide. You are face to face with one of nature's most accomplished killers.

But this hunting scene is not limited to Africa. Spiritually, this scene occurs every day in every city, town and village in the world. As a Christian, you must realize you are being hunted. Satan, the lion, stalks you. He watches you. He is crouching nearby. You cannot run. You cannot hide. The absolute horror of facing the lion is unimaginable. However, one thing is guaranteed: You *will* be stalked. You *will* face him. You *will* grapple with him. I hope you are ready—for the fight of your life!

This chapter is reprinted from *The Lion Never Sleeps* © 1996 by Discipleship Publications International. Read this book for inspiration and guidance on overcoming the enemy! It can be ordered from the DPI Web site at www.dpibooks.org.

5

Surrender and Finding the Will of God

Gordon Ferguson

Discovering the will of God for our lives seems at times to be an elusive goal. How can we determine which decisions are in keeping with God's plan for us? Much of what has been said about this topic is riddled with subjectivity and likely to mislead. The seeking of "signs" and "inner promptings" of the Holy Spirit often leads us in the opposite direction of true surrender, thus allowing "self" to reign supreme.

However, the Bible does talk about finding and following the will of God. Most of the Biblical references to the will of God are simply describing (1) his sovereign plan for the world or (2) his moral will for our lives as expressed in his word. Knowledge in either of these realms comes only through what he has revealed. Other references appear to refer to a third element: his will (or plan) for our individual lives. He does have such a plan, although we may discover it through hindsight rather than foresight!

As each of us seeks God's will for our personal lives, we need to keep a few practical principles in mind in order to avoid confusion. One, many of our everyday decisions are not highly significant in their importance. In such instances, God is quite willing for us to make any one of several choices. Two, such decisions usually are not issues of right and wrong, but rather good, better and best. Three, when our choices are more significant, the outcome of the decisions themselves are not the only factor to consider. Our personal character development should also be taken into consideration. Developing a spiritual mind-set is just as important as making the "right" decision.

In the first two categories, we should always be spiritually minded and kingdom-focused without being overly concerned about making mistakes. To worry about "missing the will of God" is fruitless. However, when the decisions are more significant in their impact on us and others, we should be much more deliberate and prayerful (but still never worried). If we are concerned enough to make our decisions in a righteous manner, God will surely lead us in making them. Philippians 3:15-16 contains a very important lesson in this regard. In essence, this passage teaches that if we are not mature enough to grasp God's will at a given point, we should continue to live up to the light we already see, while trusting God to reveal additional light as we go. It is, therefore, a question of *process* and *progress*. God often leads us within the process of trial and error. But if we remain faithful and surrendered through even the errors, he will lead us onto the path of progress of a greater understanding of his will for us.

But what does surrender have to do with finding the will of God? Simply stated, we cannot see clearly without it. Jesus said,

> "The eye is the lamp of the body. If your eyes are good, your whole body will be full of light. But if your eyes are bad, your whole body will be full of darkness. If then the light within you is darkness, how great is that darkness!" (Matthew 6:22-23)

In context, Jesus is warning against having our eyes focused on the physical aspects of life. When we are looking at the world with a materialistic (or humanistic) view, we cannot see God or his will for our lives. When we look at it with a heart surrendered to God's purposes, God is free to make his will evident to us.

As we search the Scriptures for God's will for our individual lives, we must understand at least three qualities inherent in a surrendered heart: humility, commitment and gratitude.

Humility

> Now listen, you who say, "Today or tomorrow we will go to this or that city, spend a year there, carry on business and make money."

> Why, you do not even know what will happen tomorrow. What is
> your life? You are a mist that appears for a little while and then
> vanishes. Instead, you ought to say, "If it is the Lord's will, we will
> live and do this or that." As it is, you boast and brag. All such
> boasting is evil. (James 4:13-16)

Pride causes one to be a *control freak*, a seeker of his own will and a boaster in what he intends to accomplish. Since God exalts the humble and resists the proud, such a person can be sure of the fall his pride will cause. As the text indicates, keeping a healthy perspective of one's mortality is necessary for maintaining a surrendered heart. No matter how long you may live, the end will come soon enough. The works of your hands soon will be reduced to a dim memory in the minds of the few who knew you during your brief sojourn on this earth. Therefore, in view of eternity, seeking God's way rather than your own is the only sane policy.

Considering decisions with a heart that says, "if it is the Lord's will" provides a remedy for pride. But a word of caution is in order: Perfunctory repetitions of this phrase will only add to our problems, as we perhaps fool ourselves and others around us. God, however, will not be fooled. The issue is not to *sound* spiritual in decision-making; it is to *be* spiritually surrendered to the will of God, whatever that will may turn out to be. Are you willing to make decisions about what job you will take and where you will live with humility? Are you willing to go against the grain of your natural tendencies in these areas?

As a leader in a very large church, I sometimes hear of members contemplating a decision to move to another city. Often, when the rationalizations are removed, the reasons given are shown not to be spiritual. Moves based on selfish motives weaken our moral fiber. Moves based on kingdom reasons, which always demand the element of self-denial instead of self-gratification, strengthen our spiritual character. In looking at my own life, it is amazing how making the most difficult decisions has yielded the most precious blessings, while making the comfortable, nonthreatening decisions has led to few blessings. Surrender demands a willingness to pay any price God asks.

If you are not willing to literally move anywhere, do anything and give up everything for God, you are not wanting to find his will. And you will not find it. God blesses humility. When we draw lines in our lives, refusing to lay certain things on the altar of sacrifice, we will ultimately pay a price. Either we will suffer for our lack of surrender, or we will miss out on what might have been.

The seeking and accepting of spiritual advice is a key factor in determining our level of humility. Without this element, selfishness and pride will have a bigger say in the directions we follow than we might imagine.

As I was writing this section, I contemplated a choice of how to spend my evening. I wanted to do one thing, but felt I should do another. Thus, I called a mature brother who had a grasp of both choices and asked for advice. He gave the advice I didn't want to hear but suspected was correct. I followed it, and during the course of the night, my wife whispered in my ear, "Aren't you glad we followed the advice?" Yes, I was glad, for the will of God had become clear. However, without the determination to ask and heed advice, I would have gone *my* way and missed out on a great experience that allowed me to bless others and to be blessed in the process. Humble out and allow God to direct your steps.

Commitment

> Therefore, I urge you, brothers, in view of God's mercy, to offer your bodies as living sacrifices, holy and pleasing to God—this is your spiritual act of worship. Do not conform any longer to the pattern of this world, but be transformed by the renewing of your mind. Then you will be able to test and approve what God's will is—his good, pleasing and perfect will. (Romans 12:1-2)

This passage teaches three fundamental truths regarding the will of God for our lives. One, he has such a will, and it is both pleasing and perfect. It is not simply acceptable or even good; it is best. Two, this will is often discerned through testing. This suggests that it often goes in the opposite direction of our human nature. Three, it can be known by us. The Greek word translated "approve" means "have a certain knowledge of." However, the earlier part of the text gives some *prerequisites* for knowing his will.

The first thing Paul calls us to do is to offer our bodies as living sacrifices to God. He reminds us that such a total commitment must be based on our appreciation of his mercy, for only then will we be able to offer ourselves without reservation or restriction. With the phrase "living sacrifice," Paul is surely wanting to contrast the sacrifice that the disciple of Jesus makes with that made by the people under the Old Covenant. Living sacrifices differ in several basic ways from the animal sacrifices of that first covenant, but the chief difference concerns the idea of limitations.

The animal sacrifices were limited in monetary cost. Even if an animal were expensive for an individual or family, it could be paid for and done with. Not so with a living sacrifice. These are limitless in price, for the debt of love to God can never be paid in full.

The animal sacrifices also were limited in time costs. A worshiper spent the necessary time to follow God's instructions, and after the sacrifice was over, he could go on his way singing "mission accomplished." However, a spiritual sacrifice is never finished until life ends.

The animal sacrifices were restricted in the location where they could be offered. On the other hand, the location of spiritual offerings is not in any way restricted. Worship is not limited to special buildings or to special times.

Another prerequisite for being in position to test and approve God's will is nonconformity—we are not to conform to this world. The Phillips translation renders Romans 12:2, "Don't let the world around you squeeze you into its own mold...." Disciples, although not rebellious in the normal sense of the term (with arrogance), must stand against the godlessness of the world. The key is to allow God to direct all of our qualities into spiritual channels rather than having them conformed to the world's mold. Just remember that Satan is always trying to distort otherwise good things into evil ones.

The last prerequisite in the passage is that we must undergo a transformation. The word "transformed" comes from the Greek word from which we get our word "metamorphosis." In practical terms, God is not simply asking us to make a few incidental changes; he is asking us to change fundamentally. We are to go from the caterpillar stage of living to the butterfly stage. We put off the worldly attitudes, values and practices, and through the power of the Holy Spirit, put on the godly qualities found in Jesus Christ. This is a continuing process.

Do you want to know what God's will is for your life? You can! But not without a total commitment to the spiritual life described by Paul in Romans 12. Surrender includes humility and commitment, and as we will see in the following section, it must be crowned by a continually thankful heart.

Gratitude

Be joyful always; pray continually; give thanks in all circumstances, for this is God's will for you in Christ Jesus. (1 Thessalonians 5:16-18)

We know for sure that God's will for our lives is to rejoice always and to give thanks in all circumstances. Unless we are willing to practice this truth, we should not expect to discover his individualized will. Finding out just how to accomplish this command is the challenge. As with all worthwhile spiritual endeavors, the way of the cross is the way to accomplish all aspects of the will of God. Without surrender, we can never be sure we have found such a will, and without it, we will never be recipients of the peace that surpasses comprehension.

God's will is not only for us to be surrendered outwardly; it is for us to remain joyful and thankful no matter what the circumstances. In this quality, we must be like Jesus. How would you describe him? If you were to make a list of his qualities, would you include *joyful*? Frankly, too few of us would think of him as a joy-filled person. Humble and committed, for sure; prayerful and thankful, without doubt; but more sober and somber than joyful. Why do we not see Jesus as he really was in this important area?

Our main difficulty is our tendency to confuse happiness with joy. Our idea of happiness is often borrowed from the world, in that it depends too much on outward circumstances. To be happy is to be free from any pressing problem, right? No, for the Christian will never be free from problems and challenges. In fact, by virtue of being followers of Jesus, we have volunteered for constant challenges. He said in John 16:33, "In this world you will have trouble."

Thankfully, he preceded this statement with "...in me you may have peace."

In Philippians 4:4, Paul told us to rejoice always, but he modified the command with the phrase "in the Lord." Note the contrast between life in the world and life in Christ. If we depend on the physical aspects of life for joy, we are in for a rough ride. If we depend on our relationship with God, we can remain in a rejoicing state. But even our spiritual activities and accomplishments are not to be the key source of our joy. Jesus said, "However, do not rejoice that the spirits submit to you, but rejoice that your names are written in heaven" (Luke 10:20). Spiritual focus is everything, isn't it?

Yes, Jesus was joyful. He had complete joy during his earthly sojourn, and he is able to provide us with complete joy. But only if we discover how to conform to his will. How can we be certain we are walking in his will for our lives? When we are willing to *joyfully* accept whatever he decides to send our way.

Can we know the will of God for our lives on a daily basis? Certainly—surrender! Keep in mind that knowing the will of God and being surrendered are inseparably linked. As defined by the passages we have examined, the surrendered heart is characterized by the qualities of humility, total commitment and gratitude. Do these qualities typify your life at the present time? Unless all three are yours, your surrender is suspect and your likelihood of living within God's plans for your life are diminished. Let's surrender and be blessed, confident that we are obeying God's revealed will and living within his customized will for each of our lives!

This chapter was condensed and reprinted from *The Victory of Surrender—Second Edition* © 1999 by Discipleship Publications International and is available through the DPI Web site at www.dpibooks.org.

6

We Make It Our Goal to Please Him
Seventy-Two Hours, a Willing Spirit and an Alarm Clock
Kelly Petre

With a year of Biblical Greek under my belt, I was thrilled to be finally putting it to use. Verse by verse, chapter by chapter, I translated the Gospel of John as part of my homework at a local seminary. I had begun to look forward to my morning Bible study times with a fresh sense of excitement and renewed anticipation. In my fourth week, I was gaining confidence as I methodically parsed verbs and looked up unfamiliar vocabulary. As it happens, John's Gospel is written in fairly simple Greek, and John 8:29 is no exception:

> "And the one who sent me is with me; he has not left me alone, because I always do what is pleasing to him." (John 8:29, Petre's Authorized Version)

It was this last phrase that caught my attention. I grabbed a New American Standard translation to check my accuracy:

> "...for I always do the things that are pleasing to Him." (John 8:29, NASB)

Then I reached for my trusty New International Version to see what it said:

> "...for I always do what pleases him." (John 8:29, NIV)

(I sure was spending a lot of time—and money—to learn something that anyone could understand by reading a standard English translation!) Truly the most penetrating truths of Christianity don't require advanced degrees to understand them.

How had I never noticed this verse before? More important, what was I going to do with it now that I did?

Jesus, Please

If we knew nothing at all about Jesus, John 8:29 would be enough to elevate him into a class by himself. His stated goal, as declared previously in the Gospel of John, had not struck me with the same force:

> "By myself I can do nothing; I judge only as I hear, and my judgment is just, for I seek not to please myself but him who sent me." (John 5:30)

This is indeed a noble ambition, but after all, there are others who have undertaken to please God. How was Jesus any different? What sets Jesus apart is just this: He succeeded in pleasing God—*always.* Surely no other man, including the founders of other world religions, could make such a claim.

What was the Father's testimony about Jesus to the onlookers at his baptism?

> And a voice from heaven said, "This is my Son, whom I love; with him I am well pleased." (Matthew 3:17)

And what did the voice from heaven say to Peter, James and John on the mount of transfiguration?

> While he was still speaking, a bright cloud enveloped them, and a voice from the cloud said, "This is my Son, whom I love; with

him I am well pleased. Listen to him!" (Matthew 17:5; see also
2 Peter 1:17)

Astonishing.

My Turn

When I consider my life as a Christian, I find that I have had
many reasons for doing what I have done: fear of judgment, desire
to please leaders, accountability to others, wanting to prove something to myself, concern for my example, or simply "because it's the
right thing to do." I think there is something noteworthy about each
of these motivations; but none has the
power to sustain and transform for a lifetime. I appreciate the growth that God has
allowed me to experience and the grace
that he has lavished on me, even at times
when my motives have been less than pure.
How challenging, though, to consider
Jesus' motivation in light of what has gone
on in my own heart! I suppose that Paul's
bold reminder to the Corinthians should
not surprise me: "So we make it our goal to please him" (2 Corinthians 5:9). My goal as a Christian is the very same goal that Jesus
Christ had for himself while on the earth: to please God. More than
just an exalted end, it is also the highest and most effective means to
that end.

> **Pleasing God is more than just an exalted end, it is also the highest and most effective means to that end.**

I needed to discover how I could really make this outlook a
part of my life. I started by pulling out a Bible concordance and
looking up every instance that the words "please," "pleased,"
"pleases" and "pleasing" appear in Scripture. I was more convicted
than ever, but something was still missing. I prayed to God and confessed that while I truly desired to please him with my life, I feared
that a simple decision on my part would fail to change me to the
depth that I believed was needed. As I shared some of this with my
wife, we came up with a simple but radical plan that is changing our
hearts—and can likely change your heart as well. It required seventy-two hours, a willing spirit and an alarm clock.

The plan was as follows: For three days, I set an alarm to go off every waking hour of my day. Whenever it did, I would stop whatever I was doing and think about Jesus' words: "I always do what pleases him." When possible, I would glance at the list of scriptures that I had compiled. Then I would think about the past hour, even about what I was doing at that very instant, and ask myself, "Is what I have been doing—and saying—and thinking—pleasing to God?"

One day seemed too short a time for me to really let this sink in. I can "gut out" a lot of things for just one day. Three days of this, however, left a profound impression on me.

Lessons Learned

What follows are a few of the lessons that I learned and convictions that were strengthened as a result of this exercise.

1. I am saved only by the grace of God. The first realization I had as a result of this endeavor was an overwhelming sense of my own sinfulness. When I really took stock of my thoughts and actions on such a regular basis, it was stunning to admit how many impure thoughts, harsh words, selfish impulses and behaviors that were not Christlike filled my days—and all this while I was focused on pleasing God! If ever I thought differently, it was now very apparent to me that we are dreadfully sinful creatures. How merciful God is— how patient and *forbearing*! It is by his grace and nothing else that we can be saved.

2. I am more in awe of Jesus than ever. Many things have impressed me about Jesus in the nineteen years that I have been a disciple: his miracles and insightful teachings, his compassion and strength, his wisdom and impact in people's lives. Today, however, I am more amazed by one aspect of his life than any other: the fact that he always pleased the Father. When we sincerely set out to please God with our lives, our admiration and wonder for Jesus Christ cannot help but increase many times over.

3. I already know a lot about pleasing God. Paul was able to say to the Christians in Thessalonica, "Finally, brothers, we instructed you how to live in order to please God, as in fact you are living" (1 Thessalonians 4:1). We have been instructed from the Bible about many things that are pleasing to God. Faith pleases God

(Hebrews 11:6, 10:38). Doing good and sharing with others pleases God (Hebrews 13:16). Obeying parents—and by extension, conducting our relationships in a godly way—pleases him (Colossians 3:20). Praying for leaders and for the spread of the gospel is pleasing to God (1 Timothy 2:1-4). God is pleased when we obey his commands (1 John 3:22), act from a clear conscience (Romans 14:18), take care of our physical families (1 Timothy 5:4)—and more. When we stop to consider what we already know, it is striking how great an awareness we have of what brings delight to our Father in heaven.

I am reminded of the dating advice that Randy McKean gave to my then girlfriend and me as we became the first dating couple in the Paris church. All eyes were on us in the young congregation, and our example was very important. And yet, knowing that no human being could possibly force us to maintain a high standard of purity in our relationship, he asked us what our own safeguards for the relationship would be. His only insistence was that we make it our goal to bring a smile to God's face with the way we conducted our dating relationship. That went further than anything else to motivate us to be righteous, and we have been blessed to build our marriage on a great foundation because of it!

4. I can and must grow in my knowledge of how to please God. While we may already understand a good deal about what it means to please God, there is always more to learn. As Paul continued in his admonition to the Thessalonians,

> We instructed you how to live in order to please God, as in fact you are living. Now we ask you and urge you in the Lord Jesus to do this more and more. (1 Thessalonians 4:1)

He called the Ephesian Christians to "find out what pleases the Lord" (Ephesians 5:10). And at the pinnacle of his letter to the disciples in Rome, Paul implored:

> Therefore, I urge you, brothers, in view of God's mercy, to offer your bodies as living sacrifices, holy and *pleasing* to God—this is your spiritual act of worship. Do not conform any longer to the pattern of this world, but be transformed by the renewing of

your mind. Then you will be able to test and approve what God's will is—his good, *pleasing* and perfect will. (Romans 12:1-2, emphasis mine)

As we offer ourselves to be pleasing to God, we will learn more and more about what his pleasing will for our lives really is. I have been inspired once again to turn to the Scriptures for guidance, with a renewed eagerness to find and to do what is best.

5. *The real battle for faithfulness takes place in my heart and mind.* Many of the decisions I am faced with boil down to the struggle to please myself or give to others, to do my will or God's. That we are to "take captive every thought to make it obedient to Christ" (2 Corinthians 10:5) is the real struggle of discipleship. My resolve to please God has convinced me that it is in this arena that I must devote my greatest energies. A famous theologian once said, "Love God and do as you will." While this could easily be misconstrued as a license for self-indulgence, I believe there is a lot of truth to this sentiment when rightly understood. If I really do love God, then "doing as I will" means acting in ways that are pleasing to him. This goes far beyond any list of rules I might devise; it goes right to the heart of being a Christian.

6. *No other motivation even comes close.* As I continue to feel the effects of this deliberate orientation, I am convinced that all other motivations pale in comparison. Fear is just the beginning of wisdom. Pleasing men can easily lead us astray. Following rules and programs can cut the heart out of Christianity. Seeking to please God, on the other hand, always prevails—because it fulfills the greatest commandment.

In the seven years that I have heard him preach to our congregation, nearly every sermon given by Richard Bellmor has ended with these words from Jesus' Parable of the Talents:

"His master replied, 'Well done, good and faithful servant! You have been faithful with a few things; I will put you in charge of many things. Come and share your master's happiness!'" (Matthew 25:21)

I suppose I should have made the connection before now, but I believe I am finally beginning to understand the appropriateness and power of this singular focus.

I don't know if an exercise such as I have described would be helpful to you or not. What I do know is that learning to please God in everything we do is what all Christians are called to do. One afternoon during the three-day period, I left my Palm Pilot in our car. As my wife, Dede, drove down the road, she couldn't figure out what was making the funny "beeping" noise under the seat. When she at last found the noisy device, she laughed and exclaimed, "Oh, it's the pleasing-God alarm!" Those seventy-two hours are up—but the alarm just keeps on ringing. I pray that we can all grow in our ability to answer its call, and "find out what pleases the Lord" (Ephesians 5:10).

7

Loving the Church
(Warts and All)

Jeff Chacon

My good friend Gordon Ferguson has a favorite saying that he uses to communicate the unconditional nature of God's love for us. He says, "God loves us, warts and all." Now, I do not know of a scripture that says that exactly (ever do a Bible word search on the word "wart"?), but I do believe that the phrase uniquely captures the spirit of the matter. God loves us unconditionally! In spite of how prideful, selfish, lazy, immoral, impure, jealous, envious, materialistic, deceitful or idolatrous (you know we could continue this list for a long time, right?) we are, God *still* loves us.

It is called *agape* in the Greek, and it means that God will never, ever give up on you! There is absolutely nothing you could do to him that could cause him to stop loving you. Oh, he will discipline you and allow the consequences of your sin to humble and break you, as any good father would (Hebrews 12:7), but he will never stop loving you. Remember the prodigal son? (See Luke 15:11-24.)

If God unconditionally loves me, what does this say about the guy sitting next to me at church? Yes, God loves him, but he's a sinner just like I am, and the church is full of guys like us two. When this really sinks in, you need to ask yourself whether or not you love the church—warts and all—just as God does. Or is your love conditional? Is your love for the church based on how people treat you in the church? Is your love based on how much others respect you or on how much others appreciate you? Is there anything at all that anyone in the church could do to you that would cause you to stop loving the church with all your heart? If so, then you do not love the church as God loves her!

What Is It?

The church is the bride of Christ (Revelation 21:9-27). All marriages have their bumps, but divorce is a sin (Matthew 19:9). Jesus would never divorce himself from the church—instead, he loves and cares for her as his own body (Ephesians 5:29). Have you divorced yourself from the church in your heart? Would God do that to you?

The church is the family of God (Ephesians 3:10-15). Are there any families you know that do not have regular conflict? The trouble is that many of us, while growing up, never learned how to resolve our conflicts at home, so we are now ill equipped to do it in the church. But the Bible teaches us to resolve conflicts quickly (Matthew 5:25) and completely (Matthew 18:35) so that they do not become resentments and bitter roots (Hebrews 12:15).

The church is the body of Christ (Romans 12:4-5), "the fullness of him who fills everything in every way" (Ephesians 1:23). So, how we treat the church is how we are treating Jesus himself. How are you treating him, as demonstrated by how you are treating his church? Imagine if God treated you the same way. Would he answer your prayers? Would he forgive your sins? Or would he pull his heart back because he is just sick and tired of the garbage and because he is just not going to take it any more? (Sound familiar?)

The First Century Example

Look, nobody said the church was perfect. But neither was the church that we read about in our Bible. What if you were a first century disciple in Corinth or Galatia? The Corinthian church was filled with sin and worldliness, and the Galatian church was totally legalistic! Can you imagine what it would have been like to be in those churches? Would you still love the church? Would you still believe she is from God? Would you still submit to her leadership? Would you still give your contribution? Would you still reach out to your friends and bring them to church? Would you still be a disciple, personally?

In the beginning of Paul's first letter to the Corinthians, he tells these worldly, sinful disciples, "I always thank God for you because of his grace given you in Christ Jesus" (1 Corinthians 1:4). Paul was not condoning their sin, but he loved them unconditionally. He encouraged them with this vision for them:

> He will keep you strong to the end, so that you will be blameless on the day of our Lord Jesus Christ. God, who has called you into fellowship with his Son Jesus Christ our Lord, is faithful. (1 Corinthians 1:8-9)

Thankfully, our confidence in each other comes from our confidence in *God's* faithfulness, not in our own.

What if you were a part of the church in Ephesus, Smyrna, Pergamum, Thyatira, Sardis or Laodicea? (See Revelation 2-3.) These churches were lukewarm (Revelation 3:16), tolerant of sin (Revelation 2:20) and spiritually dead (Revelation 3:1). Would you feel justified in holding back, trying just to survive instead of thrive, not giving your whole heart to the work? Or would you obey the command of Jesus to repent personally and do your part to make the church better?

After each of the challenges that Jesus gave to the seven churches in Revelation, he closed with something similar to this: "'*He* who has an ear, let *him* hear what the Spirit says to the churches. To *him* who overcomes, I will…[give a blessing]'" (Revelation 2:7, 11, 17, 26; 3:5, 12, 21, emphasis added). The pronouns "he" and "him" in these passages make it clear to us that Jesus is laser focused on each individual disciple's response to his rebuke. When God sees us, he does not see crowds, he sees individuals. How will you personally respond to the challenges in your church? Do not be critical of your group. Repent personally and help others to do the same.

What I Love About the Church

Sometimes when I get negative and critical of my wife or children, I just stop myself and begin to list the things I love about them. It helps me to be grateful and to focus on the positive (Philippians 4:8-9). I did that with the church recently and wrote down many of the things that I love about the church. Here is a partial list to help you get started on your own list:

- It saved my soul!
- It saved my son's soul (two more children to go).
- It teaches me the Bible, which saves my soul constantly.
- It teaches me how to love my wife and children, which saves my marriage and family constantly.
- It inspires me to do great things with my life.
- It has given me the best friends of my life.
- It taught me how to sing and how to cry.
- It shows me God.
- I love the sincerity and realness of the church.
- I love the idealism of the church.
- I love the conviction of the church.
- I love the multiracial, multicultural make-up of the church.
- I love how hip and "nonreligious" we are.
- I love to see and hear about the miracles that go on all the time in the church.
- I love that you can go almost anywhere and find instant family in the church.
- I love that the church is led by great men and women who help me to believe again.
- I even love that the world misunderstands, hates and persecutes us, because otherwise we would not be the real church (Luke 6:26).
- And I love watching baptisms—it is the only thing worth giving my life for (Acts 20:24).

This is a partial list. Go ahead, write your own list.

A Final Charge

Paul charged the Ephesian elders to "be shepherds of the church of God, which he bought with his own blood" (Acts 20:28). How valuable is the church to God? He paid the highest price imaginable for it—his own blood. How valuable is the church to you? Dare we devalue what God values so highly? Dare we treat as optional, unworthy of our highest sacrifice and burdensome that which God spilt his own blood for? If God sacrificed so much to redeem his church, shouldn't we sacrifice as much to be a part of it, to advance it and to make it better?

To borrow from one of the most famous United States inaugural speeches, ask not what your church can do for you, but what you can do for your church! Love the church. Serve the church. Cherish the church. Be proud of the church. Identify with the church. Be loyal to the church. Never bad-mouth the church. Always stand up for the church. Build the church. We *are* the church. Let's love the church—*warts and all*—as Jesus does!

8

Restoring Idealism
Andrew Giambarba

What life is most analogous to ours as disciples: doctors, lawyers, firemen, the bomb squad? We are involved in so many life and death decisions in the most intimate areas of people's lives and hearts. What characteristically happens to the people in those occupations: burnout, jadedness, cynicism They tend to lose their idealism, which happens to us in the kingdom in huge numbers.

God, however, is the eternal idealist. We serve a God "who gives life to the dead and calls things that are not as though they were!" (Romans 4:17). He called the emotional Peter "Rocky." He called the timid Gideon "mighty warrior." He called the fallible David "a man after my own heart."

The Bible is chock full of idealists from beginning to end. Think through some passages with me. In 1 Samuel 14:1-14 it was Jonathan who said, "Nothing can hinder the LORD from saving, whether by many or by few!" (v6). Read Psalm 18:30-42: with my God I "can bend a bow of bronze"! (v34). Hebrews 11 is a roll call of idealists: Abel, Enoch, Noah, Abraham, Isaac, Jacob, Joseph—"and I don't have time to tell of Gideon, Barak, Samson, Jepthah...." (Read v32 to the end.) "The world was not worthy of them...*Only together with us* would they be made perfect" (vv38, 40, emphasis added).

What happens to us? We go from one stage to another, progressing from

Idealist ➤ *Realist* ➤ *Cynic*

The progression in Biblical terms is from

Faith-Filled ➤ *Faithless* ➤ *Critical*
or
Servant ➤ *Leader* ➤ *Victim*

Think about these definitions.

ide•al•ism *n.* The practice or tendency of seeing things in ideal form; pursuit of an ideal; a philosophical system believing that reality consists of ideas or perceptions.

ide•al•ist *n.* **ide•al•is•tic** *adj.* **ide•al** *n.* A concept or imagined state of perfection; highly desirable; perfect; an ultimate objective; an honorable principle or motive.

ide•al *adj.* Conforming to absolute excellence. **ideally** *adv.*

re•al•ism *n.* Concern or interest with actual facts and things as they really are. **realist** *n.* **realistic** *adj.*

cyn•ic *n.* One who believes that all people have selfish motives. **cynical** *adj.* **cynicism** *n.*

In layman's terms, a cynic is interested in "figuring things out." A realist is interested in "just the facts." An idealist is interested in God.

Restoration 101

Last year Mari and I really needed God to restore our ideals. We had become realists at best...and so had the church. There was apathy towards the weak, the lost and the young. God sent Kip McKean many times to Miami, and in one of those trips the idea came up about us leading the church planting to Lima, Peru. We did not realize how much we needed God to restore our ideals, but God himself did. And so we left, took our two children and lived in a one-bedroom efficiency apartment for the summer. Three scriptures were restored to me in their idealism that summer. Maybe you cannot go to Lima this summer, but you can go with me now into the Scriptures and let God restore your ideals.

Not About Me

> "I sent you to reap what you have not worked for. Others have done the hard work, and you have reaped the benefits of their labor." (John 4:38)

One week after we arrived in Lima, we decided to have our first evangelistic Bible talk. We had no invitations; we only found a facility two days before the event. And yet, eighty-one adults were in attendance. One of the women there, Miriam, was met by my wife, Mariana. She was in her last year of architecture studies and was walking down the street. What was happening in her life was incredible—she was at an absolute crossroads, and what she decided would determine how she felt the rest of her life. And at that exact moment Mari walked into her life. Who had done the hard work? God. It is not about me!

We have this "realistic" evangelistic formula: We start with the promises of God, then we subtract a percentage based on our city and our doubt. Then we subtract another percentage based on the spiritual "perfection" of our week (i.e. how many great quiet times we had, whether or not we fought with our spouse or our roommates…). Then we subtract a percentage of just feeling like God would rather bless others, and then we end up with about twenty percent of our original one-hundred percent belief. We must take ourselves *out* of the equation. Remember this little phrase: "It is not about me!"

What about your current city of residence? Who is doing the hard work? In Lima, visitors were invited by the mission team who were the childhood friends of other disciples. A sister in Sao Paulo, Brazil, was originally from Lima. She saved up her money in order to go home to invite her best friend to come to church. Mother and daughter disciples from Los Angeles came to invite their friends from childhood. A couple from Bogotá came to take "vacation" there to help start the church. They all "found" such open people, but who was really doing the hard work?

Restored Faith

> "I know your deeds. See, I have placed before you an open door that no one can shut. I know that you have little strength, yet you have kept my word and have not denied my name." (Revelation 3:8)

Do you listen to the Lord when you pray and study? We had an all-night prayer at a lighthouse on a cliff in Miraflores. We paired up in twos and we took shifts at the lighthouse praying for the first church service. I was praying and thanking God for all that he had done, and the verse above came to me—loud and clear.

We had thirty-one disciples on the mission team and our first service attendance goal was 153 (from John 21:11!). This would be a 4:1 ratio of visitors to disciples. Then came the night before, the morning of, and God blessed us with 434 in attendance! This is a 9:1 ratio. The former vice president of Peru was there, and 199 wanted to study the Bible. It's not about me!

Are you idealistic about your goals? Are you idealistic in your evangelism, or are you shocked by the miracles? We can be surprised by our own legitimacy. If there is one thing that *infuriates* me, it is when disciples act *surprised* when God decides to work in their lives. We act like we cannot believe it when someone comes to church...and then likes it...and then wants to study the Bible...and then makes it out of the darkness! Our faith level and idealism have sunk so low. Of course there are open people because God is the one who opens a door. And if he opens it, it *cannot* be closed—believe it!

> **God, however, is the eternal idealist. We serve a God "who gives life to the dead and calls things that are not as though they were!" (Romans 4:17).**

Is Everyone There?

> When the Gentiles heard this, they were glad and honored the word of the Lord; and all who were appointed for eternal life believed. (Acts 13:48)

God already knows who is ready to go. Why am I talking so much about the lost? Because this is all you think about on a mission team. And nothing will restore your idealism faster than getting involved with the lost. There is too much about "me" in the church today.

The Peruvian President of the Welfare for the Capital, equivalent to the Surgeon General in the U.S., Came to all of our services and Bible talks. He received a phone call in the middle of my Bible talk—from the President of Peru—and he told him that he needed to call him back because he was in a Bible study. I felt so fired-up!

What am I worried about? What are you worried about? Remember the last Sunday service of your group: Is that all the people who were appointed for eternal life?

Idealists Fight

Remember Jonathan. Remember Daniel. Remember that unschooled and ordinary men changed the world.

My "situation," my "weaknesses," my "struggles"—the more we are focused on these things, the less we will fight for our ideals. We must be focused on being spiritual men and women.

This chapter was originally published on the Web site for the South Florida Church and is used here by permission (www.southfloridachurch.org).

Daily Life

9

Faithful with Finances

Jim Brown

I have good news about getting out of debt and getting on top of your finances and good news about getting back hope and a future. God says in Jeremiah 29:11, "'For I know the plans I have for you,'" declares the LORD, "'plans to prosper you and not to harm you, plans to give you hope and a future.'" This is what God wants for each one of us. He wants us to prosper in every way as disciples. He wants us to be effective in everything we do, so that everything we are a part of will make an eternal difference, either in our own lives or in the lives of others. Finances are an integral part of our spiritual lives. You can say to yourself, "I just hope my problems with debt will go away," but they will not just disappear by wishing. You can say, "I don't want to think about it," but you *need* to think about it!

What qualifies me to write on debt management? First, I am a disciple. Second, I have a background in finances. Third and most important, I am debt free. This is what qualifies me to teach.

You Must Have Finances

The most basic requirement for your finances is, obviously, that you must have some! You have to have money in order to have a workable budget. The apostle Paul had some very specific instructions about finances. Open your Bible to 2 Thessalonians 3:6-15 and follow along as I point out some highlights.

Have you ever opened up a refrigerator at a brother's house and just helped yourself? It seems that Paul would have a problem with that. Instead, he "worked night and day, laboring and toiling so that [he] would not be a burden to [anyone]" (v8). Also, he did not borrow money from any of the brothers; he had his own.

Additionally, brothers who do not work need to be warned (v15). If they refuse to work, you cannot even associate with them (v14). We are not to regard them as enemies, but we must be honest and direct with them as brothers. The Bible is very emphatic about the need for every disciple to work and to support themselves. We need to have money and for most of us, the only way to do that is to get a job. Some of us have jobs, but they are jobs that are going nowhere. I realize that there are times that we just need to get a "survival job," but for a lot of us it is time to get a degree, or to go back to school to finish a degree—so that you can get a better job.

A few of us are probably feeling a little heavy, thinking, *I don't have a job so no one is going to associate with me now!* Well, I have great news for you! I have a job for you. It starts Monday morning at 8:00 and ends that day at 5:00 P.M. or later. You will get paid nothing. I know you are wondering what kind of a job this is….It is the job of looking for a job. You are now fully employed as a job hunter. If you are single, when your roommates leave the apartment for their jobs at 7:00 A.M., so do you. When they come home at 6:00 or 7:00 after a long day's work, so do you. When they talk about how challenging their day was, you're right there with them. So, now you have a job and you can eat and associate with the body of believers. You are all united, and God will bless you.

You Must Be Financially Responsible

> "Whoever can be trusted with very little can also be trusted with much, and whoever is dishonest with very little will also be dishonest with much. So if you have not been trustworthy in handling worldly wealth, who will trust you with true riches? And if you have not been trustworthy with someone else's property, who will give you property of you own?" (Luke 16:10-12)

In this passage, God is equating the manner in which you handle money with your spiritual life. If you are not a good manager of your money, you cannot be a good manager in the kingdom. God will not give you all the spiritual riches he longs to give you if you have not first proven that you are responsible with the money with which he has blessed you. The way you handle your money is a test of your heart for discipleship, your faithfulness to God, and your readiness to be trusted with someone's soul. Let's look at four areas in which we need to prove our trust to God.

Never Cheat God

Read Malachi 1:8-14. If you cheat God, do not expect a whole lot of blessings from him. If you want to get on top of your finances and enjoy the prosperity that he brings, then you cannot cheat God. He says that you are "cursed" if you vow to give your best to him and then renege. When we became disciples, we vowed to give our best to him, our firstfruits. In other words, a tithe of our gross salary. (There is a big difference between gross and net. We tithe from the gross. After the government takes their cut, it is called the "net.") In the First World churches, we also commit to a yearly missions contribution to plant churches. Typically, a disciple will give about fifteen percent of his gross income to God. If you think that seems like a lot, consider a Jew in Jesus' time. Ten percent of his income went as a tithe to the Levites. Another ten percent went for feasts. Additionally, every three years he gave ten percent of his income to the destitute. This totals more than twenty-three percent on tithes alone. On top of that, they had offerings: wave offerings, freewill offerings, guilt offerings, thanksgiving offerings and special offerings. Then the Romans would come in and tax them heavily. So what did that leave? Not much.

Have you ever felt like you never have money? All of us can relate to that. Haggai 1:5-6 is saying that one of the reasons that this happens is because we cheat God. We think we need some or all of the money that we had previously committed to him so we hold back on giving to him. If you give to God first, you will find that God sews up those holes in your pocket! When you are really on track, you will have money and think, *Where did that come from?*

Take Care of Your Household

> If anyone does not provide for his relatives, and especially for his immediate family, he has denied the faith and is worse than an unbeliever. (1 Timothy 5:8)

This is a strong teaching. How do you measure up? Do you just go to the automatic teller machine (ATM), take out some cash and put it in your pocket without your wife knowing anything about it? This is not right. Do you go on shopping trips without anyone knowing what you bought? This is not right either. Husbands and wives need to be open with one another and communicate about money regularly. Work a discussion of finances into your weekly scheduling time. Discuss purchases with one another. One solution is to have a rule where one partner cannot make any nonessential purchases above a certain amount without the consent of the other. I have seen husbands spend money on compact discs (CDs) and sporting equipment while their wives were having trouble putting food on the table. Living like this, how are you going to get your kids through college? Get on top of your finances, and start saving right now. How about retirement? Even though we need to be living every day of our lives spiritually as if it were our last, as good stewards of our money, we need to prepare for the future in a righteous way. However, do not hold back on your contribution so you can save for these reasons. Honor God first, then take care of the future.

If you do not have a checking account, you need one. You get a great tax deduction from the government for your contribution to the church and other charitable contributions, and canceled checks are your best way to document these contributions.

Love the Brothers

> Let no debt remain outstanding, except the continuing debt to love one another. (Romans 13:8a)

In many cases, disciples' financial management is so poor that they frequently run out of money and have to borrow from their brothers and sisters. It shows a gross lack of discipline, and as we have seen from the Scriptures, if God cannot trust you with money, how can he trust you with souls? I strongly, strongly discourage any borrowing or lending of money between disciples. I realize that there are genuine emergencies when we lend without even expecting repayment. I do not mean situations like that. I mean facing the fact that you messed up and now you need to live with it. You do not need to borrow. You need to scrounge and eat the rice that has been at the bottom of the refrigerator for two weeks, or the pasta in the back of the cupboard, or the sack of dried black beans left over from a gag gift. With that kind of righteous attitude, God will sew up the holes in your pockets, you will get on top of your finances, and you will be on your way to being a success story.

Hate Debt

Financially speaking, there are two types of people: those who get ahead and those who fall behind. The difference between the two is debt. Those who get into debt fall way behind; those who have no debt get ahead. It is as simple as that!

Of course, there is such a thing as a responsible and acceptable debt, like a student loan. However, to get student loans and then not finish a degree should not be viewed as acceptable. To go in debt for school and then have nothing to show for it is foolish.

A business loan is an acceptable debt, provided the plan for your business is a thorough and realistic one. A house mortgage is acceptable debt, as long as it is within your budget and can be paid off in a reasonable amount of time. A car loan is a little less clear. It is better to buy a used car that you can afford than to buy a new one for which you cannot afford to make the payments. New cars are considered by many finance professionals to be one of the world's worst investment choices because of how much depreciation occurs during the early life of the vehicle. (And keep in mind that leases, which are growing in popularity, are just another form of debt.)

Now let's look at debt that is just plain bad: The number one offender is credit cards with unpaid balances. Oh, that golden plastic moment! Swish, swish. It makes some feel so good to hand over that credit card to get what they want—until they get the bill! Credit cards are not bad in and of themselves, but you should make it your goal to never carry a balance. My conviction is so strong about this that I have four credit cards, and I have never carried a balance on any of them. I have never paid a finance charge, and I have never paid a late fee. Credit card companies hate me. They make billions and billions of dollars on the finance charges and late fees charged to the financially undisciplined. They love people who carry balances. They send such people more credit cards. They tell these people they are preapproved! They say, "Your excellent record has 'gained' you a platinum card!" Or maybe it's a super-mega-ultra platinum card! The credit card companies try to make us feel like not accepting their offer makes us idiots. I just take all those offers and throw them into the trash where they belong!

If you get into credit card debt, you become a slave. You feel like a slave. You get discouraged and depressed. Those of you who are in credit card debt need to get out as quickly as possible. Some of us are paying eighteen to twenty percent interest or more. You are being eaten alive financially and you need to get out of credit card debt and never, ever get into it again. Many people come into the kingdom with a load of credit card debt. Some who have been in the kingdom a long time have also been sucked into this trap. Many with that kind of debt live in denial. Don't stay in denial. Get open with someone who will help you work out a plan to get that debt off your back.

It has been proven that most millionaires in America are not large salary earners or people who have inherited money. They are people with good financial habits who have put their money together a little at a time (see Proverbs 13:11). A penny saved is a penny earned. A hundred dollars not spent is a hundred dollars in savings. Jesus told his disciples that it is a godly trait to be shrewd with our finances (Luke 16:1-9). It is a worldly attitude to spend money however we want to and then get jealous of those who have money left to spend. We can even accuse people who are on top of their finances and who have money to spare of being worldly. This is not right!

We need to be shrewd spiritual men who strive for greatness in our finances. We need to use our money and possessions to advance the kingdom. A good rule of thumb is to give according to your income and live as if you only made half of it. Remember that no matter how much debt you are carrying, you can conquer it with the power of God (Matthew 19:26). Be hopeful; be excited; and never give up! You will be victorious!

Condensed from material originally published in *A Saving Faith: A New Look at a Disciple's Finances* © 1998 by Discipleship Publications International. This book is available through the DPI Web site at www.dpibooks.org.

10

Still Eager for Discipling
Rick Luz

In the formative years of our movement, many of us were excited about discipling. We may have had a few fears, but on the whole, we were zealous about having people involved in our lives and getting the help we needed to change and grow. In one sense, we may never fully recapture the feelings of those early days, but we can still be eager for discipling. For me, this is another way of saying "I'm still eager to grow and become like Jesus." The literal meaning of the word "disciple" in the New Testament is "a learner." Disciples then are those who are constantly learning how to become more and more like Jesus. Of course learning to be like Jesus is not just gaining knowledge, but rather, becoming like him. This principle is found in the last half of the Great Commission and should be applied as much as the first half: "and teaching them to obey everything I have commanded you" (Matthew 28:20).

Long-Term Learners

We need to continually learn how to become more like Jesus. This takes concentrated effort and does not just happen by being around spiritual people, by going to church or by being a member of God's kingdom. One principle that is often repeated in self-improvement and leadership literature is to never stop learning. As disciples of Jesus or "learners," we absolutely need to have this attitude. Given our subject matter—Jesus, the King of kings, Lord of lords, God in the flesh, Creator of the universe—this will take a lifetime of learning! Learning to be like Jesus is exciting and the most fulfilling purpose in life. It is the greatest of all human endeavors. It will never leave you empty or struggling with the feeling of, "What should I do next in life?"

If we each want to maintain our spiritual edge, it will take us remaining students and having a hunger to learn and grow. Track and field champion Jackie Joyner-Kersee said, "I maintained my edge by staying a student—you always have something to learn." As we get older physically and spiritually, this attitude can elude us because we can feel there is not too much more to learn. Our life experiences and our basic knowledge increase as we age, and it becomes more and more tempting to become set in our ways. I became a disciple when I was a teenager and am now thirty-six years old. In all of those years I have heard my share of sermons, classes and workshops. I have been part of countless discipleship times, discipleship groups and leaders' meetings. It is tempting to think, "I have heard it all before" and to not be excited about learning, growing and changing.

Most people, as they mature, lock into a rut and plateau out. I am reminded of Ecclesiastes, where we are admonished: "Remember your Creator in the days of your youth...." (Ecclesiastes 12:1). The passage goes on to describe how we might make excuses as we get older and let circumstances control us (Ecclesiastes 12:2-7). Why does the Bible say this? The Lord knows that as we grow older, our hearts are less receptive and open to change. It does not mean that it is impossible for more mature people to change and grow, but it becomes more challenging as we grow older. Therefore, we should guard our hearts against complacency and take responsibility for our own spiritual growth.

Sometimes we can look at the Christians around us and compare ourselves to them and lower our personal expectations. They become our excuse for not growing and learning to be more like Jesus. On the flip side, we can become other people's excuses. When other disciples observe your life, are they inspired to grow to become more like Jesus, or does your example make them satisfied about where they are spiritually?

If we don't make a conscious decision that we are going to grow, the routines and challenges of daily life will choke out our growth. We will lose our hope and idealism and became satisfied with where we are, becoming complacent and even cynical.

One of the many blessings of being a disciple is that we can continually grow and change.

> And we, who with unveiled faces all reflect the Lord's glory, are being transformed into his likeness with ever-increasing glory, which comes from the Lord, who is the Spirit. (2 Corinthians 3:18)

The main purpose of discipling is to help us to grow to become more like Jesus—"to be conformed to the likeness of his Son" (Romans 8:29). This is the very thing that all of us want to do deep down in our hearts. If we desire to grow and be more like Jesus, God has provided many ways for us to do this, and discipling is one of them.

Discipling Dynamics

In our lives discipling takes on many forms, and God uses many methods of teaching and encouraging to help us grow to be like Jesus. Here are a few key ways.

His Word

God disciples us directly through his word. Each time we open up the Bible, God is communicating to us and wants to disciple and teach us to be more like him, to be more like Jesus. This is exciting to think about! In Hebrews 3:7 and 10:15, the Hebrew writer quotes Old Testament passages from Psalms and Jeremiah respectively and begins by saying "the Holy Spirit says" and "the Holy Spirit also testifies to us." When the Hebrew writer read the Scriptures, he knew it was God in the form of his Holy Spirit talking to him. When we open the Bible today, it is God's Holy Spirit communicating to us. What an amazing thought! Have you ever thought, "I wish I could talk to God and have him communicate back"? The Bible contains the very words of God and contains everything he needs for us to know; it is thorough and complete, as God says in 2 Timothy 3:16-17.

How are your discipleship times with God going? Do you go to God with the areas that you need to grow in the most and thoroughly study what he has to say about them in his word? Are you being discipled by God through his word? I have recently been going through a relationship challenge in my life that I needed to bring to God. I got up at 4:00 A.M. and listened to God by reading about Joseph, David, Daniel and Jesus and how they reacted to relationship challenges in their lives. This helped me to have a proper and spiritual perspective on my situation.

As a young disciple, I had a very self-condemning attitude, and I felt like the worst disciple in existence. I took this to God and wrote my negative thoughts down and found scriptures to correct these thoughts. I put these scriptures on index cards, and every time throughout the day that I had a self-condemning thought, I would look to God for discipling by pulling out a scripture like Romans 8:1, "There is now no condemnation for those who are in Christ Jesus," and I eventually realized that this included self-condemnation. Going to God and listening to and learning from his word changed my life and continues to change my life.

Life's Circumstances

God disciples us through circumstances. He uses hardships and sufferings to disciple us and help us to be more like Jesus.

> We do not want you to be uninformed, brothers, about the hardships we suffered in the province of Asia. We were under great pressure, far beyond our ability to endure, so that we despaired even of life. Indeed, in our hearts we felt the sentence of death. But this happened that we might not rely on ourselves but on God, who raises the dead. (2 Corinthians 1:8-9)

Paul and Timothy felt so much pressure and anxiety that they despaired even of life. But God allowed these circumstances in their lives to teach them to be more like Jesus by relying on his power and in turn to help others who will go through similar struggles. Paul and Timothy must have been reminded of Jesus in the garden of Gethsemane (Mark 14:32-36) and his ultimate trust in God's power and surrender during a time of great distress and suffering. Do the hardships and challenges in your life teach you to become more like Jesus, or do they reduce you to being self-reliant and to having a worldly perspective?

Do you take your challenges, frustrations and hardships to God first, before you seek the encouragement of others? The older I get, the more I realize that God is and always will be our only source of unfailing and unconditional love, strength, support, hope and encouragement. People have failed me in my life; leaders and other disciples have hurt me and have greatly disappointed me; but God is constant! No circumstance can ever take this away from you or me.

> One principle that is often repeated in self-improvement and leadership literature is to never stop learning. As disciples of Jesus or "learners," we absolutely need to have this attitude.

Others

God disciples us through other people. Part of God's amazing design for his people is the body of Christ, the church. When we are baptized, we are baptized into the body of Christ, the church. We become a member of God's household or family! (See Ephesians 2:19.) It has always been part of God's plan to use men and women to help each other find him and to encourage one another to become more like him and his Son. From Genesis to Revelation there is one account after another of God using people to instruct and encourage one another.

As a movement, we have decided in most situations to apply the Biblical principle of discipling in one-on-one discipleship partner relationships. Although such an approach is not commanded or directly exemplified in the Bible, it is a very acceptable way of applying the discipleship principles. With our busy, distracted, modern lifestyles, many people will not get the help and encouragement they need if we choose some less organized approach.

These relationships work best when they are horizontal, as I believe God intended, instead of vertical relationships. By this I mean there needs to be a great deal of mutuality. When there is an emphasis on one man being over another, the relationship can quickly become unhealthy and dysfunctional. The relationships that have worked best for me are those in which an open, healthy family atmosphere is present and we are able to talk to one another man to man about anything that is on our hearts and that we see or feel.

If we have been in the kingdom for any length of time, we have all no doubt experienced the benefits of one-on-one discipling relationships. However, we can't let our concept of discipling relationships end there, and we should not allow ourselves to be limited in this way. Discipling is not sitting down one-on-one with someone, waiting to get all your needs met. Sometimes we look to one person to solve all our problems when we have a whole spiritual family around us. This is unscriptural and will lead to unhealthy expectations that no one person can live up to. There is not a soul alive who has all of the characteristics and qualities of Jesus.

Besides our discipleship partners, we should also look to the men and women in our Bible talks or whatever small group our ministry is broken down into at the time. A great source of personal growth is available via every disciple around you who has unique strengths and qualities.

In addition, we should look to previous discipling relationships. I have been in many different regions and groups within the church and currently have many relationships that I have maintained and continue to receive inspiration and encouragement from. Each of us should choose several people who help us the most to become more like Jesus, and that we have the same impact on, and work on those relationships during our lifetimes.

It is not fair for anyone whom you disciple to expect you to meet all their needs or for you to expect the person discipling you to meet all your needs. I personally have never expected the men discipling me to make me grow. The Bible says that we must work out our own salvation with fear and trembling (Philippians 2:12) and that we must train ourselves to be godly (1 Timothy 4:7).

In light of this, another great source of discipling that I have relied on is being discipled by many of my heroes in the faith like Kip McKean, Al Baird, Randy McKean, Sam Laing, Scott Green, Frank Kim, Jim Blough—and the list could go on and on. I have barely met some of these men and have spent very little time with the rest. How, might you ask, have I been discipled by all of these great men and more? Through their lessons, sermons and books that

I have consciously sought out. Since these men have unique qualities, strengths and wisdom that we cannot expect all of our discipleship partners to have, we can grow and become more like Jesus through their teaching.

Constant Growth

There is no limit to how much each of us can grow. It will take us a lifetime to touch the hem of Jesus' garment as far as attaining to his life and character. However, with his help, grace, mercy, patience and kindness, and with each other's help and a lot of grace, mercy, patience and kindness, we can all reach our full potential in Christ.

11

If We Don't Stick Together

Steve Johnson

Before Calvin died I got one more phone call. With his kind of cancer we had long stopped praying that God would make him better. We just prayed that it would please be over for him soon, thank you, Jesus. Next thing you know you're getting the phone calls.

"The doctors say that radiation won't help anymore."

"This is it. They just give him a few more days to be with us."

"I know you're busy but could you come down and see him in the hospital?"

Life seems so long, and all of a sudden it's only a few days and a bunch of phone calls.

I went down and sat by him on one of those beds that you never want to think about ending up on yourself. I don't remember much about that talk, only that when I left I knew I'd never see him again.

A couple of days later I got another phone call from his wife, Joyce.

"He's asked them to turn off the IV."

Calvin's IV was an electrolyte and nutrient cocktail meant to prolong his life. He had asked to speak to his doctor alone, without Joyce, because he wanted to know if he would ever go home again. The doctor said no and that his IV was keeping him alive. Calvin said to turn the thing off.

"Are you okay?" I lamely asked Joyce over the phone.

"I thought I was ready but I'm not. How about you?"

"Me? I'm fine, it's just...."

"Just what?"

"I made some reservations to fly down and see him again."

I hung up, knowing that in the next few days I'd be getting that other phone call telling me that it was time for the funeral. But not five minutes later the phone rang.

"Steve, can you come on down here now?"

The irony that we had been on the phone just seconds before and now he was dead choked me until Joyce calmly spoke again.

"I told Calvin that you had plans to come see him."

"Yeah?"

"He told them to start the IV back up."

The Bible says that greater love has no man than to lay down his life for a friend. But what do you call *refusing* to die so you can see somebody one more time?

So our last conversation was about a friend who had decided to leave our fellowship.

"He just doesn't get it," Calvin said. "If we don't stick together, we'll never make it."

Submission Is Powerful

I believe Calvin made it, and the legacy he left me was a vow to unity, a vow to stick together, to "get it."

One of the secrets of the universe is this: *Voluntary submission is powerful.* In Ephesians 5:21 ("Submit to one another out of reverence to Christ...") Paul commands us to give in to each other. Not an easy thing for mortals, but then he motivates us with the nudge "...out of reverence to Christ." He doesn't say to submit to another brother or sister only when they are being spiritual giants and Biblical geniuses. He simply says to submit.

If we could see submission like a traffic intersection with a four-way stop then maybe we could understand that God commands us to yield in order to avoid bad accidents. Everyone eventually gets a turn when everyone submits to one another. This creates unity and unity provides the climate necessary for the Holy Spirit to do his work.

Nothing has demonstrated this principle in the church more than our experience with Hope for Kids. Originally an immunization drive in Orlando, we found a niche for serving in the metro New York area by knocking doors and reaching out to folks who don't usually have assistance getting their children immunized.

The story would have ended with one successful weekend project in Harlem if not for the unity among churches across America. In one year's time Hope for Kids went from being an outreach in one city promoted by three thousand volunteers to a coast to coast campaign more than thirty thousand strong. Hope for Kids then was able to make such a splash that corporations and official health organizations have been eager to partner with us in helping children in nearly every state of the Union.

Because disciples of Jesus are willing to be united and work together, Hope for Kids has become what Bud Chiles, Hope for Kids director of New York, called "the Ford Foundation with teeth." We're united. We show up. We don't quit and we're not afraid to work for others. And we want God to get the credit.

Just as our flesh is tempted in many ways to be arrogant and proud, divisive and cynical, our spirit longs to be righteous and united in eternal pursuits. I'm as likely as anyone to get a bad attitude when someone's desire to boss me around clashes with my opinion or seems to be speeding toward a head-on collision with common sense.

But how can we honestly think we have any chance at living forever with God in heaven if we can't live with each other for just a little while here on Earth? We need motivation for the times when we don't feel like participating in something "bigger than ourselves" or when someone is not leading just the way we think they should be. We need to remember Jesus and submit to each other on our "bad hair, bad prayer" days. We need to be able to think of the people who have sacrificed for us and be inspired to get moving and do something for someone else.

For me, motivation is pretty easy. I can think about Calvin—how he wouldn't die until he'd seen me one last time just to talk about unity.

Just to make sure before he left that I "got it."

Reprinted from *Hope for a Hurting World* © 1997 by Discipleship Publications International.

12

You Can Make Disciples
Jack Frederick

Since my baptism just after the crust of the earth cooled, I have maintained a deep conviction and desire to reach out to friends and family. God, with kindness, has given us lots of fruit and great friendships. During the past twelve months, he has blessed us to see ten friends baptized into Christ. These are ten people met personally by me, my wife, Gail, and my children, Steven and Anna. Our other daughter, Sarah, and her husband, Michael, were away leading the church planting in Sarajevo, baptizing others.

Such stories are challenging to us average schleps who work fifty-plus-hour-per-week jobs, maybe have a wife and kids, like to fish or play golf and enjoy watching *The Simpsons* (d'oh!)—or lesser intellectual stuff on PBS! Even to those whose job is the ministry, meeting ten people who become disciples is a challenge.

Let me pause here for a reality check and to honor God to whom all credit is due for any good thing. We work hard evangelistically, and I am grateful he blessed us, but all of us are unworthy servants at best (Luke 17:10). I hope my family can inspire you to be as unworthy as we have been and as joyfully fruitful. Just remember: don't tell your friends what *Jack* did, but tell them what *God* did—I get in enough trouble with pride without you aiding and abetting me.

Keeping your evangelistic focus and learning how to be effective in your evangelism are crucial because those around you are

78

depending on you to bring life and light to their lives. God "wants all men to be saved and to come to a knowledge of the truth" (1 Timothy 2:4). He will do his part as we do ours.

Convictions Are Critical

What are your convictions about making disciples? What motivates you to keep your evangelistic focus? Some basic convictions have kept me zealous about this for many years, but making these convictions my own required determination on my part. How did I gain convictions? I watched others. I walked with them. I served them.

I am an engineer, but don't fit the stereotype very well—I tend to be less structured and like to fly by the seat of my pants. I have had to change "who I am" to be a disciple and to be a more mature man of God. I was neither born nor reborn as a man of deep convictions, but have tried to become so. I wanted to capture Jesus' heart of seeking and saving the lost (Luke 19:10).

Be a Man of Gratitude

Initially, I did not relate to the great men in the Bible, but I felt a bond to the wild demoniac of Luke 8. Growing up, I usually wore clothes, but I connected to his isolation. I grew up monetarily challenged, the son of a single mom and was shy, withdrawn and generally ignored by others. What stood out to me about the first disciples I had contact with was that they wanted to know my name. How many people do you imagine asked this demoniac's name? Maybe they shouted it over their shoulder as they ran away back to the synagogue. I dare say the man had never heard the words, "What is your name?"

> They sailed to the region of the Gerasenes, which is across the lake from Galilee. When Jesus stepped ashore, he was met by a demon-possessed man from the town....
> Jesus asked him, "What is your name?" (Luke 8:26-27, 30)

This is why I feel such gratitude to God. He could never ask me to do anything that I consider "too much." Look what he did for me! He spoke to me in public when I was not cool. He sat down at my table. His social status took a dip when people saw him with me. Do you consider this as you have people into your home or reach out to them, whether they are disciples or the lost? Solomon writes, "Whoever is kind to the needy honors God" (Proverbs 14:31). How have you been honoring God lately in this way?

The Gerasene madman across the water brings me next to my most difficult change as a young disciple.

Conquer Timidity by Your Gratitude

> For God did not give us a spirit of timidity, but a spirit of power, of love and of self-discipline. (2 Timothy 1:7)

As a junior in college, I had been on three dates in my life, all after graduating from high school. And each date precipitated a throbbing headache from the stress. For me "shy" was a gross exaggeration on the positive side. But when a brother later showed me this scripture, I was convicted. (What? Like I could've pretended I was not timid?) I would go with him to do what we called "face to face" on the campus, accosting strangers to share our faith with them. I couldn't speak up, but I watched. After a year of this (and my friend's graduation), I was like Bill Cosby's 1960's comic sketch on karate: I would always take the toughest cases—people the seasoned veterans were afraid to invite.

Remember, it was not my courage but my faith, conviction and love for the Savior who wanted to know my name. Don't waste your breath on excuses about being timid. I had to overcome it, and *he* showed the same kindness to you as to me, no matter who you are or who you were.

Be Eager to Change and Grow

In a small church in New Zealand, the song leader opened a window to let in the breeze. In the back of the small auditorium a little old lady yelled, "Shut that window!"

Later, the evangelist told her, "You can't talk to people like that."

She replied, "That's just the way I am."

The wise preacher replied, "There is only one I AM; the rest of us are to become like *him*."

Don't be content to be "just the way you are," but become like Jesus. I have been trying to become more and more like him for three decades. I was not a man of conviction before I became a disciple, but I changed. I turned fifty in January and last night I watched the video of my family and friends sharing at my birthday celebration. Most poignant was my wife's sharing. She shared two scriptures from which she says I have never wavered: Matthew 22:37-38 and Matthew 6:33. I don't think she mentioned this to me in all our years of marriage until my birthday party. Gail had watched me measure the changes in my life by these scriptures to see if I was becoming more like Jesus. I changed and so can you.

Love One Another and Love People

Jesus tells us that all men will know we are his disciples because we love one another (John 13:34-35). I have listened to my favorite sermon ("Christian Love" by Mid McKnight) more than two thousand times. I need lots of coaching on this. It takes prayer and practice for me to be loving. It takes learning from others and from the Bible about the things we do not excel in. Nothing is more important than love, as Jesus said in Matthew 22:37-38. If you are not known for your love, find someone who is and spend time with him. Attach yourself. Become like him. Imitate.

Serve and Show Hospitality

Once, when we had lived in the Boston area for several years and had been leading the children's ministry for our region, at eleven on Saturday night, the new, young evangelist phoned me to ask if I would give the message before the Lord's Supper the next day. His first choice had cancelled. It was a "homecoming service," and we had invited everyone who used to be a part of the church but had fallen away. To relate in my message, I shared about being disfellowshiped from a large traditional church a few years earlier (another story for another day). In sharing, I asked how many in the audience had been in our home for a meal, and three-fourths of the eight hundred raised their hands.

Frankly that shocked my wife (and me, too), but this kind of hospitality draws people into the family of believers. It helps people to be baptized and to form close bonds between brothers and sisters.

It gave us a chance to get to know people, to learn from them and to imitate them. We have had homeless people over. We invited Bush, Clinton and Ms. Twain but they haven't accepted yet. But E. J. Murphy and Rollie and Arlene came. The blind and the lame have been here, and certain angels unawares (Hebrews 13:2 KJV). We have shared our hearts and home with all these and learned from them all.

Don't Show Favoritism

Wear blinders (James 2:1-4). Reach out to everyone, not simply people who are like you. Share with old and young, all races, all economic backgrounds—you get the idea. And don't simply share with them; open your heart and your home. Gail and I have always invited people home from church, rich/poor, older/younger, leaders/the weak, friends and critics, too.

Yearly, it seems, Gail and I baptize someone who is more than seventy years old. I love studying with older men and women. Our daughter Anna, 19, baptized four friends from her high school during the last year, plus one of their moms and another mom is now studying.

Here are some other examples of people my family and I baptized with the help of our Bible talk. George is a young African American who was homeless during his teen years in Alabama. Dennis is a fellow rocket scientist who has worked with me for twelve years. James is another African American, a chief in the Navy at MIT. He, his wife and nephew were each baptized last summer.

Remember that you need your Bible talk (the village) to raise (study with and disciple) all these children (1 Corinthians 12 and 13).

Shamelessly Imitate Others

My family and I have made the most of opportunities and challenges in our lives to learn from others. We are convinced that we grow most by spending time with others who have strengths we wish to imitate. For example, I repaired Wyndham Shaw's car and boat in order to spend time with him. (Then he took me fishing!) Gail has prepared sumptuous meals for the other leaders after church or for Thanksgiving or Christmas. The fellowship is great, but so are the learning opportunities.

When I travel on business, rather than taking a spiritual vacation, I make every effort to spend time with disciples. I invite evangelists and their wives out to dinner with me. Lane Houk once took me and my teen son tarpon fishing in Tampa; then I brought visitors to their congregation. In Tokyo in 1987 George and Irene Gurganus invited me to stay with them. I gave up a luxury hotel room, opting to sleep on tatami mats in George's humble abode, but what a treasure! Once, while in Los Angeles, I dropped by the Kingdom News Network (KNN) studio to visit Roger Lamb and was privileged to have dinner with the Lambs and the KNN anchors from Hong Kong and their adorable baby (way prettier than Roger!). In Tokyo and Sarajevo I hit the streets with new disciples to share my faith, and I learned from them. Each of these experiences has left a mark on my character.

While away with coworkers, share with them and take them to a Bible talk or to church. Get to know the local disciples where you travel. Away time doesn't have to be down time.

I have tried to imitate good things I see in others. I find my speech affected by the people I am around, though I can't yet articulate the Somerville, Massachusetts, accent like my friend, Phil Arsenault. I shamelessly adopt ideas and habits from brothers and sisters wherever I go.

Watch Out for Distractions

Many good things will take our focus away from being evangelistic. Below is a partial listing of distractions, all of which may be commendable in and of themselves. This is where we should seek good, objective discipling and input.

- Work/Career—travel, competition, money, technology, rocket science, toys, business trips
- Family—Gail and my children, sex with my wife, being family, meeting needs, enjoying them, teaching them, traditions
- More Family—mothers, kinfolk, brothers, sisters, in-laws, aunts and uncles, grandparents
- Hobbies—working on automobiles, working on the house, the yard, music, tapes, computers, palm pilots
- Church—training others or myself, teaching classes, teen ministry, preteen ministry, counseling, children's ministry, serving as elder/deacon/evangelist/other

- Relationships—friends, neighbors, community, politics
- School/College—post-grad stuff, on-going education
- Fun—sports, vacation, holidays

Your family is the most important spiritual responsibility God has given you. Your job is important to God (Ephesians 6:5-8). Friends and family make up people to whom you devote an evangelistic focus. Church responsibilities take time (notice that the church list is the longest! Heresy?). I need to be a great elder/shepherd, but I need to set an example to the flock in reaching the lost (1 Peter 5:3).

Get input in order to forge a good balance, but don't let good things become an excuse for neglecting Jesus' last words, "Go make disciples."

Wrap It Up!

My convictions have driven me over the years, and you must seek to gain convictions of your own. As I write, my nephew from Los Angeles is making guacamole. I always wondered what they put in that stuff that made it so great (and I can't get good guacamole on the East Coast). He is sharing the recipe with me. I have shared with you how to stay focused on the mission of reaching the lost, but you must remember that you can't just add these ingredients and expect great guacamole. You must put these things into your heart. You can learn quickly, but don't try to make this a microwave meal. As Peter says:

> For this very reason, make every effort to add to your faith goodness; and to goodness, knowledge; and to knowledge, self-control; and to self-control, perseverance; and to perseverance, godliness; and to godliness, brotherly kindness; and to brotherly kindness, love. For if you possess these qualities in increasing measure, they will keep you from being ineffective and unproductive in your knowledge of our Lord Jesus Christ. But if anyone does not have them, he is nearsighted and blind, and has forgotten that he has been cleansed from his past sins. (2 Peter 1:5-9)

Borrowing from Amos, I am neither a prophet nor the son of a prophet. I am an engineer and suffer the weaknesses and derision that most engineers face. I work long hours and travel frequently. I have a wife, three children, a son-in-law and a foster daughter. I serve as an elder and bear my region's burdens "to fulfill the law of Christ" (Galatians 6:2). For years we led the children's ministry of 250 kids and fifty teachers, plus a Bible talk and a family group. My wife has taught elementary school and had other jobs outside the home, plus cooking, cleaning and making her husband very happy. My kids played soccer, T-ball, basketball and more.

But Jesus said, "Go, make disciples," and we can all do it with his help.

13

When the World Looks Good

Thomas Jones

Being in the kingdom of God in this world is an amazing experience. Yes, there are challenges, but there is no doubt in my mind
that this is the way, the truth and the life. And, yet, I must admit that
there are times when the world, or at least something it has to offer,
looks good. This is largely what temptations are all about. I know I
am not alone; we are all tempted. When we become disciples, we see
through a lot of the world's appeal, but there are still times when
something about the world looks attractive to us all.

Something to Appeal to Everyone

We have an enemy who tailor-makes his schemes for each of
us. This means that the appeal of the world is going to come to us in
different ways. Something that is attractive to me may not bother
you at all and vice versa. But from time to time, *something* will come
along outside of Christ that looks very appealing to us all. For most
of us there was something that brought us comfort or pleasure
before we became Christians. When the heat gets turned up on our
discipleship or when disappointments, fatigue or our doubts have
an affect on us, some of those things may suddenly seem very
appealing again.

From time to time I gave gone to a cabin in New Hampshire to
write. I must tell you that life there—far away from the phone, the
distractions and the disruptions—begins to look very good. Each

time I go, I find it a bit hard to pack the bags and leave that some-what isolated spot and start back for the Boston suburbs, knowing that needs and problems in other people's lives await me there, as they always do. When I stay there, I can look across the way and see another property where the owner of a nice year-round home has a canoe, a sailboat and a ski boat. It all looks pretty appealing.

> **The truth is, there is a more comfortable life you could be living, but there are things more important than comfort.**

When I shared this with my friend, Gordon Ferguson, his comment was an inter-esting one: "Oh, I know. If I were not a disciple, I would definitely live some place like that, far away from most human inhabitation." Now, you personally may not be tempted at all by the things that tempt older guys like us. You may be the kind of person who goes nuts if you aren't right in the middle of a bustling urban area, but this I know: *There is something about the world that will at some time start looking good to you.*

It can seem sometimes that our commitment to Jesus is inter-fering with "the good life." If I was not spending so much time reaching out to others and attending so many meetings, I would have more time to do X, Y and Z. If I was not giving so much money to the kingdom, I would have enough left over to buy this and that. Joe Christian walks out of his house on a Sunday morning, through his yard he hardly has time to mow and gets into his seven-year-old Toyota. He sees across the street his neighbor's shiny new SUV, observes his well-manicured lawn, and looks a bit enviously at him coming out in his shorts to get the morning paper—the first act in a day of sheer relaxation. Or Bill Christian leaves his apartment in downtown Metropolis and sees his neighbor lacing up the roller blades for a day of cruising through the park. We cannot deny it: there are moments when the world looks pretty good.

The attraction of the world is especially powerful when you personally are being opposed for your faith or when the church is not in favor in your community. The world also starts looking better and better when you are going through some struggle to change your character, and there are disciples in your life bringing you some strong but needed challenges. Such change means hard work.

From somewhere you hear a voice saying, "There is a much more comfortable life you could be living."

Consider the Whole Story

The truth is, there is a more *comfortable* life you could be living, but there are things more important than comfort. The writer of Psalm 73 fully experienced what I am describing here. Before you read on, take your Bible and read what he wrote.

You can see that he looked at his unspiritual neighbors and wondered out loud if they did not have it better than he did. "In vain have I kept my heart pure," he groans (v13). In other words, "I have worked hard at being what God wants me to be, and it looks like other people who don't care about God have it better than I do." But then he did what we each need to do. He went to worship (v17) and something happened in that experience that reminded him of "the final destiny" of those who do not seek or love God. There are snapshots of the lives of non-Christians that look good. Here they are roller-blading carefreely on a Sunday morning. Here they are in their sailboats. Here they are, taking off on another weekend get-away. Here they are building yet another new house. But these snap-shots do not represent the whole picture.

First, there are all kinds of things going on behind the scenes. If non-Christians have it so great, why do so many of their mar-riages end in messy divorces? Why are so many of their kids doing drugs? Why are so many singles running ads in the paper that read "Attractive SWM looking for female companionship"? We must not be faked out by outward appearances. "The good life" may be only skin deep. When you probe a bit, you find it isn't so great. Surely some of us can remember this.

But then, there is the issue that the writer of our psalm brings up: *their final destiny.* Even if life in this world were better for the non-Christians (which it is not), there would still be the issue of the final destiny. And "final" destinies are final, irreversible and perma-nent. If we love the world now, we may get some temporary pleasure, but there will be a final destiny where we will lose it all. There will be times when the world looks good. It has strong appeal to the natural man. There will be times when it seems life might just be better if we were to let go of all this radical commitment to Jesus.

At such times, we need to worship. We need to see God clearly. We need to remember that we have been redeemed from an empty way of life (1 Peter 1:18). We need to see that man apart from God is but dust (Psalm 103:14), a fading mist (James 4:14) and grass that withers (1 Peter 1:24). We need to sit down and make a list of all the blessings we each have in Christ that we would lose if we left him. The truth is, whatever we give up to follow Jesus, we can afford to give up! What we get by being his disciple, we cannot afford to lose.

> Do not love the world or anything in the world. If anyone loves the world, the love of the Father is not in him. For everything in the world—the cravings of sinful man, the lust of his eyes and the boasting of what he has and does—comes not from the Father but from the world. The world and its desires pass away, but the man who does the will of God lives forever. (1 John 2:15-17)

This chapter was adapted from *Letters to New Disciples* © 1997 by Discipleship Publications International and is available through the DPI Web site at www.dpibooks.org.

14

Working with Leaders
Thomas Kuhn

It seems appropriate to begin this chapter by telling you a little bit about who I am so that you will better understand my perspective. I have been "around" the discipling movement since approximately 1980. In those days many of us were a disjointed group of people trying to be disciples (some more successfully than others) and waiting for someone to pull it all together. At that time, I was a young married professional man living with my wife, Carma, in Morgantown, West Virginia. Through a series of moves and adventures that only God could write the script for, I am now living in Palm Beach County, Florida, a forty-eight-year-old software engineer with three children, Rebekah, Rachel and Tommy, who are disciples. My beautiful wife and I will be celebrating our twenty-fourth year of marriage in just a few months. I serve currently as an elder for the South Florida Church of Christ with John Brush. Through the years, I have had the privilege of working with and being led and discipled by many different men, so I am looking forward to sharing with you about the subject of working with leaders. Hopefully, even through some of my mistakes, you will gain fresh insight about approaching the subject in a way that pleases God.

Perhaps you are a young disciple and find yourself not exactly sure how to properly submit to your leaders. After all, this is what the Bible calls us to, right? Hebrews 13:17 says to obey your leaders, to submit to their authority, and to "obey them so that their work will be a joy, not a burden, for that would be of no advantage to you." Does this mean to do everything they say without question? How do I work out differences? How do I maintain the right attitude? Or maybe you are a spiritually older disciple, and well, come to think of it, maybe you have the same three questions! Seriously, though, you may have some things to work through that you have been afraid or unwilling to approach. Let's look at some basic principles.

Understand Why You Are Who You Are

The first principle is mainly for the older ones among us. Are you ready for it? Here it is: *You are where you are by the grace of God and nothing else.* I have had literally hundreds of relationships through the years with people whom I have led and been led by. Some I have done well with and some I have totally blown. It is very important that you never start looking at your achievements and begin to count them as a product of your own good heart. Once I start doing this, I start moving from the realm of being teachable to being stiff-necked—this is not a good place to be! God will oppose this kind of person.

I believe that this is the greatest challenge for those of us who are older. As I age, I find myself fighting more often the battle of wanting to dig in and be entrenched and stubborn about an idea that I have or "the way things ought to be, according to me." Paul said it best in Philippians 3:7-8:

> But whatever was to my profit I now consider loss for the sake of Christ. What is more, I consider everything a loss compared to the surpassing greatness of knowing Christ Jesus my Lord, for whose sake I have lost all things. I consider them rubbish, that I may gain Christ. (Philippians 3:7-8)

This scripture applies just as much to our achievements in the kingdom as it does in the world. Yet, we can begin to think we know a few things, and then we start looking down our nose at a young leader, and one thing leads to another, and then you have a bitter older disciple, a frustrated young leader, and a relationship that has reached an impasse.

I have literally done so many things that God could have chosen to deal with so severely, but instead, over and over again, he has shown me his infinite grace and mercy. So, I am where I am today in spite of myself and not because of myself. If we keep this on straight, we will be able to approach those who lead us with a proper, humble attitude, not a defensive posture. Actually, I have found this to be the most effective antidote for bitterness there is. Whenever I am counseling older disciples, the scripture I "live in" the most is Hebrews 12:10-11, followed by verse 15. At every stage of life, God disciplines us in some way. We have a choice to make every time: either we accept the discipline, no matter how painful it is, or we reject it, in which case we will end up in bitterness, which will defile not only us, but our families and others around us.

Do Not Make Assumptions

The second principle is certainly for everyone, but will be especially useful for those of you who are younger: *Do not make assumptions*. I have had to learn this one over and over again as the years go by. I am very good at putting scenarios together in my head of what may have happened or could have happened. Unfortunately, a lot of times they are dead wrong! My family has had great sport in pointing this out to me when they catch me doing it. They are determined to have me deal with it—and good for them! If you do not understand why a leader makes a particular decision, ask for an explanation. And there is a right way and a wrong way to do this. Do not come to them demanding to know why something was done. Remember Hebrews 13:17. Ask respectfully, with phrases such as, "Can you help me understand what your reasoning was when…?" You will grow very quickly with this simple change of heart. You will also find yourself not just doing things because someone says so, but with an understanding of the reason and heart behind it. This is certainly the principle followed by the disciple in Luke 11:1, who simply asks, "Lord, teach us to pray, just as John taught his disciples."

Work Out Differences

The third principle I would offer is huge: *Work out differences.* This one is for all age groups and all situations. I am convinced that the number one reason why people fall away is relationship issues.

This can be Satan's biggest area of victory, or if it is approached spiritually, it will provide a glory to God unlike anything the world around us has seen. In fact, this forging of relationships is one of the main reasons why the movement of God remains united today and has been able to succeed in accomplishing the goals that have been laid out by its leaders. We can be so afraid to work things out. Do you know why? We are afraid to find out that we might be wrong about something and worse yet, to have to admit it. These are the same reasons why people leave families and refuse to speak to one another for years. The threat of it is constantly brewing in the kingdom of God, but you can make a decision to not let Satan have his way with you.

A second reason why working things out is hard is because of the fear of being hurt. What if the other party does not want to talk things out? What then? Then you get help. You get a mediator. But frankly, 99.9% of the time, this is not necessary. Most differences come from a failure in following the second principle above, not making assumptions.

However, there are cases in which relationships need to be hammered out over time, and it can be a painful process. Let me give you some hope here. The longest running relationship I have had since I have been a disciple has been with Jeff Chacon. We have been together now for six years. I have served as his disciple, Bible talk leader, zone leader, sector leader, shepherd and elder during that time. He has led a church and led regions during that time. Through it all, we have been together. Yet, we are very different people. He would say, laughing, that there are many times that we have taken turns driving each other crazy. However, during those years, I have learned more than at any other time. I believe that he would say the same thing. If I could sum up our natural bent, it would be that I can be removed, heartless, calculating. Jeff is very feelings-oriented and sometimes sentimental. Yet I can say, weeping even now, that he has taught me more about the grace of God than any other man. He has changed me forever, and I will always remember this no matter where we find ourselves. I know that he would also be able to tell you about the things he has learned from me. So, this can be the result of following this toughest, but I believe most crucial, principle. I have had other relationships over the years when I have not worked things out and they did not turn out as God had intended them because of my lack of spirituality.

Honor and Respect Your Leaders

The next principle involves adopting "a new attitude"! *Simply stated, give honor and respect to your leaders.* This involves some thinking that is exactly opposite of how the world thinks. Think about the relationships with leaders that you are able to observe in your workplace, school, neighborhood clubs and associations. What is the common factor you almost always see? It is a disdain of leaders. Critique is constantly going on behind their backs, whether they are accomplished or inadequate. Perhaps you have participated in these critiques. Satan loves this! He hates authority. He will use any tool he can to tear it down. I believe that any leader, regardless of talent or ability, can be successful at leading if people make a decision to get behind him. In a given group, office division, football team, or whatever, I believe it can come down to the decision of one person to follow the leader that will ultimately make or break the leader. If you are that person, and you make that decision, you will be the leaven that changes the group. This glorifies God!

When my children were smaller, one of their favorite Bible passages (particularly for my son, Tommy) was 2 Samuel 23:13-17, when three of David's mighty men break through enemy lines to get a drink of water from a well just because—just because David wanted a drink and his men wanted to honor him. What incredible hearts! What nobility! Doesn't that just thrill you when you read it? I am sure it thrilled God when he saw it being played out! God loves this kind of depth and love in relationships.

What about 1 Samuel 14:6-14? Jonathan decides to attack the Philistines and his young armor-bearer says, "Do all that you have in mind. Go ahead; I am with you heart and soul." How thrilling that statement is! There is no tentativeness. No suspicion. "I trust you completely" is what he seems to be saying. "My life is in your hands."

Believe me, I understand being wise and weighing advice and all of those things. But I also believe that we must have deep loyalty toward our leaders. Frankly, when the world walks into our fellowship and sees this, they are blown away by it.

I remember a few years ago when I was going through a rebellious stage in my Christianity. I was just not doing well spiritually and did not want to be in submission to anyone. Fortunately, my good friend, Alex Hull, who was discipling me at the time, latched onto me and would not let go. Through thick and thin he stayed with me, whether I wanted to see him coming or not. When I finally repented, I just wanted to honor him and Pree, his wife, in some way. I remember the Sunday night when Carma and I were sitting together talking and decided we would go to the grocery store, buy a bag of their favorite foods, show up at their house and cook the Hull family dinner. We did, and it was a joyous night with lots of tears. This was the beginning of a very fruitful time in our lives, as God saw our genuine repentance and responded to it.

Leaders Are People Too

I hope that by reading this, you can capture a heart for what you need to be for the leaders in your life. Leaders need friends. They need people who will lift their arms up (Exodus 17:11-13). God is joyful when he sees this kind of heart. The world is blown away by it. Let's all decide to have a new heart in this area. We will teach the world much by showing them how we love each other, especially those who lead us (John 13:34-35).

15

Overcoming Anger
Ryan Howard

One day a seemingly mild-mannered, loving disciple was criticized by his boss. That was the last straw. He went back to his office, punched a hole in the wall and broke his telephone. His boss often criticized him in front of others. Later he confessed, "I got to the point where everything he said aggravated me. I became super-sensitive, super-critical. I justified slandering him behind his back. As the frustration built, I felt helpless and powerless to stop it. I thought it needed to come out. After the explosion I felt terrible....After I lose it, it just sucks the guts out of me. I hate feeling out of control. I know it destroys my relationships. I just feel like dirt."

This same brother will go home, and if he feels the least bit of criticism from his wife, he will defend himself, argue awhile, then clam up for the rest of the evening, deliberately not talking to her, camping in front of the TV for several hours. He names his main sins as laziness and selfishness. Yet this is a classic picture of being controlled by anger. Whether expressed openly (aggressively or passively), it is blatant malice. You hurt me, I hurt you.

This is not an unusual scenario, even in the kingdom. You might say, "I've never done that." But remember that Jesus says, "Anyone who is angry with his brother will be subject to judgment" (Matthew 5:22). The problem is, few of us realize we are angry until after we have sinned.

When we made Jesus Lord and were baptized, forgiven and set free from all our past sins, God said sin should no longer be our master (Romans 6:14). We saw that anger was a sin from the Word; we confessed it; and we may have thought that all the anger from our past was gone and would never again be like it was. Or maybe we have just come to realize that we have an anger problem.

Sins like anger were conceived far in our past. After baptism, when anger continues, we become confused, asking, "Am I really a disciple?" Like our brother above we feel terrible, ashamed and embarrassed to tell anyone—yet all the while, we feel justified. Or we blame it on others—my boss, my job, my wife, my roommate, my teen, my discipler—"They make me angry." We feel trapped. But good news: this is all a part of God's molding of us and his revealing that only his power can overcome our weaknesses. God takes all the anger, sin and damage done and works it together for good to make us strong, fruitful men of God, humbled by this truth. Only his power can overcome our anger.

What Is It?

Anger is a God-given emotion. Jesus had it, but he used it righteously. Satan has twisted it in mankind so that it has continually led to the destruction of nations and individual lives. What was given to Adam as a powerful brain chemical to be used to fight off evil was adapted by Satan to destroy relationships. Anger shows up as:

- dirty looks
- frustration
- sarcasm
- threats
- hostile humor
- irritability
- knotted muscles
- many words
- faster–paced words
- accusations

or it can also manifest itself as:

- name calling
- provoking
- swearing
- hitting
- belittling
- pointing fingers
- yelling
- injuring
- slamming
- throwing
- trashing
- murdering

Unrighteous anger destroys. But in Christ, we are more than conquerors, able to overcome any sin, no matter how deeply rooted it is. He will teach us to say "No" to the anger that destroys relationships and develop in us righteous anger that defeats sin (Titus 2:11-14).

Why Do We Get Angry?

> A wicked man puts up a bold front,
>> but an upright man gives thought to his ways.
> (Proverbs 21:29)

God has created us with needs. We all need to be valued by God and by others; we have basic needs: sleep, food, physical safety; and relational needs: companionship, communication, cooperation, sexual fulfillment in marriage. When these needs are not met, we can protest in our own minds and become angry. For example, we may think we do not get the attention or help we need, and immediately feel irritable. We need love, but we must learn not to react angrily when we do not get it. We must stop allowing our emotions to be determined by external circumstances.

A precious few of us grew up in the type of family God intended for us to have. In Deuteronomy 6, God makes it clear that he wants Dad and Mom to love him with all their hearts, to love each other (Matthew 19:4-6) and then to love their children. This is God's desire and expectation. When this does not happen while we are growing up, we, as children, resort to getting our needs met in worldly ways. Additionally, insecurity develops instead of confidence; sexual sin rather than self-control; manipulation and demands that others love us instead of confidence that God meets our needs; fear instead of commitment; isolation instead of opening the secrets of our hearts; control instead of surrender to God; or in some, a hopelessness that these needs will never be met. Often anger turns inward, which leads to depression.

We also become angry when we feel as if someone is dishonoring or being insensitive to our personal convictions. Think of the many violent social protest scenes in history. Often it is a kind of righteous anger that eventually spins out of control. For instance, I can pride myself in my style of leadership in my family. When my wife and children do not comply, I get angry. Also, I may have strong opinions about what needs to change in our Bible discussion group to make it more effective, but the leader might not listen to me. These situations can cause our anger to erupt. And the more dogmatic we are, the more easily angered we are.

A brother shared with me that he was angry for years, not realizing that his anger was stemming from fear. Now, instead of being overcome with the anger that arises from unmet expectations in his family, he asks himself the question, "Wait, what am I afraid of?" He went on to say, "When my kids would act up, I finally realized I feared for them spiritually, that they would not turn out to be disciples." This fear drove him to want to control his children and make them meet what he saw as God's expectations. Sadly, his unrighteous anger defeated the very goal for which he longed and prayed. Identifying his fear reminded him of God's promise: that faith and love will drive out fear.

My story is similar in many ways. The fear that arose when my children misbehaved, especially in front of other people, ignited anger in me toward them. My desire to be seen as a model father with a perfect family, and my subsequent guilt when I felt as if it did not materialize, proved to be Satan's scheme to destroy my family. I became a critical judge. I found myself shaming instead of loving my children, which exasperated and discouraged them—and my wife. It hurts to even recall those years, but God has redeemed me by his forgiveness and empowered me to overcome the fear and anger that ruled my heart.

In a recent conversation with Al Baird, whose work takes him to many churches, he remarked that he has seen in kingdom families that anger in the father is often revisited in the son. "When the dad gets angry, there is no way for the kid to plug in. The father's anger destroys communication, to where kids may leave, saying, 'My folks never listened to me. They didn't really care what I thought. There's no sense talking to my dad because he sees things his way.'" He continued, "You can repair the relationship only by changing and showing him you've learned to listen, asking him for his help to be a sounding board and to say when you don't feel listened to. If you can get through to the level where he starts talking to you, then you are over the hump."

How do you express anger? How did your dad or mom? How did they respond when you were hurt, sad or angry? Could you talk? Did you feel understood?

Al's words describe what happened between me and my teenage son, Joe. Though I deeply love and respect him, our anger (mostly mine) had almost destroyed our communication. But, by God's grace, with both of us taking responsibility for our sin, we have overcome and our bond is being repaired as I practice the suggestions you will find at the end of this chapter.

> **Anger is a God-given emotion. Jesus had it, but he used it righteously. Satan has twisted it in mankind so that it has continually led to the destruction of nations and individual lives.**

"He [Jesus] knew what is in a man" (John 2:25). Therefore, would he not want us to understand our anger as he does? Mark it down: Emotions of fear, sadness, loss, hurt, loneliness and inferiority are often precursors to many forms of anger. Unmet expectations and guilt are powerful triggers in situations in which angry feelings overcome us. I am not talking about psychologizing or navel gazing, but examining ourselves to find out what sets us off. Then we can take hold of the power of God's truth to overcome.

Our Way

> "In your anger do not sin": Do not let the sun go down while you are still angry, and do not give the devil a foothold....
>
> Do not let any unwholesome talk come out of your mouths, but only what is helpful for building others up according to their needs, that it may benefit those who listen. And do not grieve the Holy Spirit of God, with whom you were sealed for the day of redemption. (Ephesians 4:26-27, 29-30)

In short, the way I speak can grieve the Holy Spirit both within me and within the other person. How have you felt when you have been within earshot of someone belittling or raising his voice at another? It is disturbing, whether observing as a stranger or as a family member. When I realized that this is how I sounded and how I made everyone around me feel, much less God's Spirit, I was motivated to change. God's way of overcoming anger is by not allowing anything out of my mouth that does not build up or bring resolution. Otherwise, my anger becomes emotional and verbal abuse to the precious ones in my life (Proverbs 12:16, 14:17).

Often in our efforts to control anger, we allow "unwholesome talk" to hammer away in our minds. We beat ourselves up internally. A brother told me that his lifelong anger problem had finally erupted, and after arguing defensively, he withdrew, scolding himself with berating self-talk. "You're such a jerk!" "You haven't changed!" "You'll never have a good relationship." "What's the use?" But these are Satan's lies. These kinds of statements are nowhere to be found in the letters written to baptized disciples. The truth says, "I am God's son"; "He's at work to change me"; "I am holy and blameless"; and "God has lavished his grace on me."

Overt, aggressive anger is easy to identify—especially by those around us! Suppression and passive aggression are subtler. Suppression is putting on a front and pretending that we are not angry, holding it inside, not "lowering ourselves" to expressions that are crude and hurtful. This style is popular among disciples who believe anger is wrong. These people keep antacid companies in business. Ulcers, backaches, headaches and God knows what other physical complaints can result. How hard it is to laugh while unresolved turmoil rages in the heart.

Passive aggression is an indirect expression of our irritation, disagreement or hurt. Examples abound: not answering the phone or returning calls, "forgetting" to do what your wife asked you to do, procrastinating, hostile humor, sarcasm, half-hearted involvement, pouting, sulking, tactfully slandering, refusing to speak to or acknowledge a person and many other Satan-devised behaviors.

God's Way

> Since, then, you have been raised with Christ, set your hearts
> on things above, where Christ is seated at the right hand of God.
> Set your minds on things above, not on earthly things. For you
> died, and your life is now hidden with Christ in God. When Christ,

who is your life, appears, then you also will appear with him in glory.

Put to death, therefore, whatever belongs to your earthly nature: sexual immorality, impurity, lust, evil desires and greed, which is idolatry. (Colossians 3:1-5)

But now you must rid yourselves of all such things as these: anger, rage, malice, slander, and filthy language from your lips. (Colossians 3:8)

Therefore, as God's chosen people, holy and dearly loved, clothe yourselves with compassion, kindness, humility, gentleness and patience. Bear with each other and forgive whatever grievances you may have against one another. Forgive as the Lord forgave you. (Colossians 3:12-13)

To overcome anger God's way, we must have God's perspective. First, take your mind back to your baptism. What did you feel about your sin? What did you feel about Jesus suffering with your own sins upon him? How did you feel when you came up, all wet, out of the water? I felt relieved and hopeful. How about you? Free? At peace? Fired up? For several weeks after I had been raised from the dead, I did not feel irritated by the criticisms that came my way. I did not feel the need to defend myself anymore. I knew I was a sinful man and that my anger hurt Jesus and others. Yet, because he forgave me, I was inspired. I had no basis to be critical of others because Jesus forgives them too. Those initial feelings were real, but as time passes, Satan schemes to get me caught up in my anxiety and anger. Now I rely on God's word to motivate me, which commands me to set my mind on Christ, his death and my death at baptism. I am convinced that if he returns today, I will be with him in glory. Therefore, I am motivated to catch my irritated, angry feelings before I say or do something sinful.

Centuries ago, Jesus asked the question, "Do you want to get well?" (John 5:6). I'm asking if you want to be free from anger's control. I did. I assume you do too, but the road to overcoming involves much openness, accountability, soul searching, hard work, and above all, hungering for the word of God and devotion to prayer.

This is what changed my life, along with my daily confession of any episodes of anger, whether great or small. Further, my wife and I completed a twenty-six-week Christian-based course to help us to better understand the roots of our anger and to change our bad communication patterns.

Many of us have been defensive our whole adult lives and have gone to great lengths to avoid facing the pain of our unmet needs from childhood. Additionally, it is hard to face the guilt from our chronic anger and the damage done to those close to us. Yet, the amount of effort and prayer determines the depth of change. Think about how you currently spend your time: in the gym, in front of the television, working on your golf swing, watching movies, helping others, eating. But in essence, God is asking you, "What is more important than these activities? Isn't working to overcome anger more important?" He promises us that it is worth the effort (1 Corinthians 15:56-58).

Remember when Adam and Eve disobeyed God. They became ashamed and afraid. Back then Cain and Abel learned sin from their parents and also watched them deal with their fear and shame. Somewhere along the way, Cain learned that it was okay to hold on to his anger. When God confronted him on his offering, he was downcast, brewing with hatred and feeling sorry for himself. Then God asked Cain directly to be open before the sin overcame him. Cain apparently refused, and anger became rage, and rage became murder.

Some In-the-Moment Practicals

"In your anger, do not sin" (Ephesians 4:26). A close friend of mine reminded me that anger rises up in all of our hearts, but the key is controlling the anger and not allowing it to control you (Proverbs 16:32).

- When you first feel angry about being slighted, cut off in traffic or feeling disrespected, pause and control your impulse. This is "the pause" that you must take, or else temptation will turn to anger, then to all types of sin. In other words, give yourself a spiritual time-out.
- Take deep, slow, abdominal breaths. Consciously relax/stretch your muscles. If possible, remove yourself from the situation.

Take a walk. Physiologically, the "anger" brain chemical activity subsides as the minutes pass.

- Identify the feeling behind the anger—give it a word. Understand what hurt you, what scared you, what insulted you.
- Honestly admit what you feel to God.
- Ask the Spirit for control.
- Realize that your enemy, the devil, wants to twist your anger into sinful reactions, but God understands your weaknesses and the weaknesses of your offender.
- Picture yourself stabbing this monster of anger to death.
- Recite several strengths of the other person and thank God for them. Go back, extending the grace to your offender that God has given you. Do or say something kind.

A Long-Term Spiritual Plan

The following is a suggested approach to help you begin your journey of changing the anger in your character.

- Give permission to family members or roommates to point out whenever you hurt their feelings.
- Take spiritual time-outs when your first angry signs appear. Pray intensely.
- Daily share any angry thoughts and reactions with a brother for several weeks. This helped me tremendously (Hebrews 3:12-13).
- Confess to God and accept his forgiveness (1 John 1:9).
- Meditate daily during your quiet time, realizing that only Jesus can meet your needs, calm your fears and heal your hurts.
- Memorize promises.
- Pray.
- Accept that your anger is usually a reaction from unmet needs and/or recent hurts or fears.
- At the end of the day, write down specific feelings and thoughts you had when you felt angry.
- Decide today to be "quick to listen, slow to speak and slow to become angry" (James 1:19) with the strength and love of Christ's spirit within you.

Fight the Good Fight

We cannot change the anger in our past. God forgives and forgets. Praise God! We cannot overcome anger in the future, nor in the next hour or year, much less the rest of our lives. Like faith, overcoming is not a possession you keep forever, but rather, a response, temptation by temptation, to the promises and presence of the Spirit in your heart.

Sexuality, Marriage

& Family

16

Purity in an R-rated World
Kevin McDaniel

Answer: Fred and Wilma Flintstone. Question: Who was the first married couple we ever saw in bed together on television? Wow, if this is really true, as I read somewhere, then we have morally regressed exponentially during the past thirty-something years. Television and Hollywood have slight regard for your morality. *As the World Turns. Days of Our Lives. Three's Company. Soap.* Howard Stern. MTV's *Spring Break. Undressed. Baywatch.* Jerry Springer. WCW. WWF. All are *bad.*

A war is being waged against your heart, mind and soul. You cannot go to the video store without being attacked by views of scantily clad women on the covers of countless movies. You cannot check out at the grocery store without seeing someone dressed in a "tini-mini-bikini." You cannot pick up a prescription at the pharmacy without being confronted by the magazine rack, either in an aisle or as you leave. What would have been considered pornography thirty years ago is now splashed across the cover of most popular publications.

Automobiles. Alcohol. Cigarettes. Furniture. Food. Restaurants. It seems that you can just name the product or profession, and it is being proliferated, promulgated and promoted with sex. The World Wide Web can be just exactly that—an international web, snare or trap. We can get entangled and later we are spiritually killed, then consumed. Now, at the touch of the keyboard, you can pump into your home the most hideous, destructive, naked trash from around the globe. Never has it been easier to be sensually and sexually impure than it is right now.

Some of us take a very casual, a very "hakuna matata" sort of attitude toward our sensual, lustful temptations. We think to ourselves "Everyone does it" or "I don't lust as much as I used to" or "I am making *some* progress." Or perhaps you have given up altogether. Jesus said for good reason,

> "If your right eye causes you to sin, gouge it out and throw it away. It is better for you to lose one part of your body than for your whole body to be thrown into hell." (Matthew 5:29)

Jesus understood the results of self-indulgent sensual behavior. We think that there are no—or merely light—consequences. We think little of how our lusts distort our perception of love and compromise our chances for a healthy relationship. We have a misshapen view of what a great friendship with a woman or wife should be. Our ideas of romance and marriage are too often a by-product of images we have assembled from the media over the years. Do not despair, however—God has a plan. Simply put: Victory at all cost!

So, whether you are married or single, young or old, you have a choice. Go to war for your own purity, and live. There is no *in between*, no middle ground. If you retreat, you will be overrun. If you hide, you will be found. If you are quiet, you will be found out. If you are indifferent, you will be destroyed. If you are *halfhearted*, you will slowly be consumed. Stand up like a man—a real man—and make a difference in your life, in your generation and in the generation next.

Got the Picture?

> "You have heard that it was said, 'Do not commit adultery.' But I tell you that anyone who looks at a woman lustfully has already committed adultery with her in his heart. If your right eye causes you to sin, gouge it out and throw it away. It is better for you to lose one part of your body than for your whole body to be thrown

into hell. And if your right hand causes you to sin, cut it off and throw it away. It is better for you to lose one part of your body than for your whole body to go into hell." (Matthew 5:27-30)

Jesus is painfully clear on the subject of our personal purity. Obviously, he goes to extreme to make his point; yet there is no doubt as to what the point is: Stay sexually pure at all costs! Here are a few more God-inspired thoughts on the subject. The world has "given themselves over to sensuality" and "every kind of impurity, with a continual lust for more." But you were taught "to put off your old self" (Ephesians 4:17-24). There should not even be a hint of sexual immorality, or of any kind of impurity, in our lives (Ephesians 5:3-7).

Do you not know that your bodies are members of Christ himself? Shall I then take the members of Christ and unite them with a prostitute? Never!

...Flee from sexual immorality. All other sins a man commits are outside his body, but he who sins sexually sins against his own body. Do you not know that your body is a temple of the Holy Spirit, who is in you, whom you have received from God? You are not your own; you were bought at a price. Therefore honor God with your body. (1 Corinthians 6:15-20)

Okay, we could go on (Galatians 5:16-21; Leviticus 20:10-21; Proverbs 5:1-6, 6:25-35, 7:24-27; Romans 1:26-32; 1 Thessalonians 4:1-8; Revelation 2:20, 21:6-8), but we will stop here. Got the picture?

Chasing After the Wind

"Chasing after the wind" is an expression from King Solomon in Ecclesiastes 2:10 that encapsulates the deception of sinful sensuality. These lusts promise fulfilling satisfaction, but they do not and cannot ever deliver the goods. For example, Solomon denied himself nothing that his eyes desired. He wrote, "I refused my heart no pleasure" (Ecclesiastes 2:10). He did not watch it on Pay Per View—he did it. Yet he concluded about sexual pleasure (and many other worldly pursuits) that they were all "meaningless, a chasing after the wind" (Ecclesiastes 2:11). Many of us understand what this means. We have lusted over what we have seen in Playboy or Penthouse. We have masturbated. We have secretively viewed XXX-rated videos. We've self indulged. Some have ventured into a city's red light district and sampled the harem for hire. We have watched the late night movies on cable and felt the emptiness and guilt of our actions. Our conscience rightly screams, "This is torture. This is meaningless. This is a chasing after the wind!"

Some of you are sinning sexually in your marriage. And yet you are too embarrassed and too "macho" to admit your need for help. Some of you are dating or hope to date one day. Listen: you are a guy who has lived in the world. You come fully equipped with all the excuses you need to blow it with your purity. "We don't go all the way, so it's okay." "It's okay because we are getting married soon." "We'll repent after we get married." "We don't need to confess to man because we confessed to God." "God made me this way. He knows I have needs that must be met. So, it's okay."

Well, guys, it's not okay because only one passage is needed in the Holy Scriptures to make something true, right? James 5:16 tells us to "confess your sins to each other." If you are single and have been using some of the above excuses or some near or distant cousin to them, or if you are married and have been concealing your transgressions with or without your wife's knowledge, then pick up the phone right now and call the brother whom you think will have the most righteous response to your sin and confess.

We will pause here until you get back. It's okay; we can wait until you have had time to be completely honest about your sin. Do not rush the conversation. I wrote this article months ago and do not need you to finish reading it for me to finish writing it. Plus, I believe in you. You can do this. I am pausing right now with tears in my eyes and emotion welling up in my heart to pray for every brother who is struggling with this challenge, as I too have struggled with it. Know that I, too, must continue to overcome the pride that stops my openness.

A few weeks before writing this chapter I, by my own initiative, sat before the regional elders that I work closely with and openly confessed my sin. I shared the things in my life "that if I fail to make it to heaven, here will be the reasons why." Impurity numbered prominently in the list. They are good men, strong brothers, faithful friends. They help me and they inspire me. They make me want to be a better man for God. Then, two weeks later, I shared on a Sunday morning what I had shared with them, in appropriate detail, in front of 500 people. Yes, that's 500 living, breathing, listening people. Surely you can handle what I have just asked you to do. Go ahead. We are pausing now. (Pause.)

Well, that was pretty awful wasn't it? If you are like me, however, it hurt "real good." Hey, man, other than the cross, you just made the "gutsiest" move I've ever seen. I'm proud to call you "brother." Stop chasing the wind.

Reaping the Whirlwind

We must either follow God's plan or pay the price. The world has solutions for the relationships between men and women. Some of them even sound good to us, but be careful (Colossians 2:8). The true answers we seek are spiritual and the mechanics of relationship dynamics alone can neither solve our problems nor meet our needs. First, let's just say that there are no benefits to recreational sex or sensual lusts. That is, there are none, *nada*, nil, zero benefits to sex of any kind outside of God's plan for it in marriage. Now, perhaps you have heard or even thought yourself that God's plan is not working so well. Just look at how many marriages fail in this world! "Look at the problems I am having in my own marriage." Is that not proof that God's plan for monogamous sex in marriage is outdated and doesn't work? Well...no. If you think that the only purpose of marriage is sex then you might have a point.

However, God created sex for two people in a marriage who share a common commitment to Jesus Christ (Ephesians 5:21-33). This commitment includes the great blessing of a sexual experience that is reserved solely for a husband and wife. God's plan for marriage is far more all-encompassing than just sex. The Bible, describing marriage and the strength of spiritual relationships (marriage and others), counsels us about submission, love, respect, care, trust, protection, honor and patience. We are warned about being rude, self-seeking, easily angered and keeping a record of wrongs (1 Corinthians 13:1-8a). Those who wholeheartedly embrace God's full counsel on the subject of marriage will build a strong relationship. So, to say that God's plan for sex is not working is foolish! God created sex for two people who are married, who love each other and who are committed to Jesus Christ. His plan works.

Of course, there are other alternatives. One of them is commonly referred to as "living together." Co-habitation has become very common nowadays. There are more than four million couples in the U.S. currently living together—ten times what it was in 1960. Is this a good solution? The median duration for these relationships is 1.3 years. That is, they "divorce" rather quickly. Some would argue that this is positive, because at least they found out they were not good for each other before they were married. Well, tell that to the millions of aborted children produced from these encounters. Tell that to the millions of kids who will never know one of their parents or at least never know them well. (Forty percent of those who live together have children.) Personally, I have not met anyone who has left these adventures without scars, damage and/or bitterness. Plus, this philosophy often leads to many more "divorces." The studies on this subject are frightening. Those who live together enjoy sex less than their married counterparts and are much more apt to divorce if they one day get married (so it's not good training for marriage after all). Also, assault on women is sixty-two times more likely with a live-in boyfriend versus a husband and, and, and….

> So, whether you are married or single, young or old, you have a choice. Go to war for your own purity, and live. There is no in between, no middle ground.

Some "play the field," and others have participated in extramarital affairs. The medical issues alone regarding this kind of behavior are of great consequence. Do this and you can lose your life from disease (AIDS). If you don't lose your life, then you are highly likely to contract a sexually transmitted disease (STD). I have read that in 1960 there were two STDs: syphilis and gonorrhea. Today there are twenty-five STDs, and one in five Americans between the ages of fifteen and fifty-five have one. Promiscuity has a price. Chlamydia and gonorrhea can cause sterility. Human papilloma virus brings on genital warts and can lead to cancer. I am no expert on these subjects, but know this: if you chase the wind, you will reap the whirlwind.

Forget all the scary info I just mentioned and hear this: Sexual sin hurts everyone. I have been in the ministry for about fifteen years, and I have seen the pain with my own eyes, over and over. And I have experienced the pain firsthand as I confessed to and sought advice from some spiritual brothers years ago and then talked to my wife about looking at pornography. She wept. She wept hard. We both felt pain and guilt.

How many of us have lost self-respect because we gave in again? How many of our children have caught us watching something we should not watch, and we had to talk to them about it? Or perhaps they caught you, and you don't even know about it? How is that going to affect their spiritual growth? How has your lust damaged the sexual experience you have with your wife? Are you making love to her or to someone you saw on the television or in a movie? God alone has the plan for your sexual life. Follow his plan and reap the winds of change, growth, fulfillment and good, old-fashioned fun.

An Ounce of Prevention

Paul wrote in 1 Corinthians 10:13 that God does not allow us to be tempted beyond what we can bear. In fact, he provides us a "way out" so that we can stand up under temptation. Sometimes the way out is not to find the way in. An ounce of prevention can go a long way. Here is some quick, practical advice for avoiding temptation.

One, don't watch late-night television or cable alone. Go to bed; you need the rest. You have to work in the morning. There is too much junk on late at night. What are you doing, staying up when your neighbors, your wife and people three time zones away are already asleep?

Two, if you are married go to bed at the same time your wife does. There are multiple benefits here. I am sure you will figure it out.

Three, understand the chronology of biology. Most impurity can be avoided in the early stages when it is easier to stop. We are built sexually to get increasingly excited. As I vaguely recall, the Apollo space missions could still be aborted with about seven seconds until blastoff. However, once this threshold was passed, the launch could not be halted. Someone at Mission Control would even say at around three seconds that "we are committed." Recognize the early signs of arousal while you can still *stop*! For many who are dating, just being alone with your date or girlfriend can be stimulating. If so, share this with a brother and avoid these times. Plan your dates to protect yourself and the sister. Don't engage in long times of kissing. If you are red-blooded and male, then you are going to get aroused doing this.

Four, set up roadblocks to sin, the best being openness and confession. If you are single, talk with a brother after a date with a sister you find attractive. If you are married and having some problems, make sure that there are close married couples in your life who can help you with your struggles.

Tap into the Power

No matter "how bad" you have been, and no matter what has happened in your past, God can and will forgive you. He is rich in mercy and wants to lavish it on you. I want to challenge you to make a decision, a pledge to God. Regarding your purity, decide to be a man of *power*.

P: I will be *pure.*
O: I will be *open.*
W: I will be a *warrior* in prayer.
E: I will live it out *every* day.
R: I will *respect* the women in and around my life.

By the power of God, you can be pure in an R-rated world.

17

Overcoming Sexual Enslavement

Mike Newman

"A ddiction" is a popular catchword these days. One frequently hears about drug addicts, sex addicts and food addicts. It seems we have accepted the term because we recognize that certain problems are very difficult to overcome and a person's will to stop does not always seem to ensure victory. The world generally considers problems that have addictive and compulsive aspects to be diseases that cannot be controlled. Some scientists are actively looking for causes to these problems in our genetic makeup. Others look at enslavement to sin as a problem of willpower rather than an issue of surrender. This overlooks the fact that we are powerless in ourselves to defeat our sinful natures. The strength of our will is completely dependent on our connection to God.[1] It is both pitiful and sad to see the lengths men will go to in an attempt to explain human moral failings without consulting God's word. The more problems we try to solve by our own wisdom , the more perplexing our problems become.

A Spiritual Issue

I am not against scientific investigation. I have two advanced graduate degrees, and I believe in research and study. I agree that there are genetic and biological factors that affect people's ability to

---

[1] The book, *Boundaries,* by Cloud and Townsend, helped me to understand how willpower is strengthened by God and relationships (Grand Rapids: Zondervan, 1992).

function. However, my own Biblical study and experience have led me to the conclusion that "addiction" is not the best term to use to describe chronic struggles with impurity. It is more accurate to talk about "enslavement" to sexual sin. Our problem is not that we have a disease, but that we are enslaved to sin.

The Bible makes it clear that a battle is currently raging between the Holy Spirit and our sinful nature for control of our souls. Either one or the other will win. Paul defines the problem as follows:

> So I find this law at work: When I want to do good, evil is right there with me. For in my inner being I delight in God's law; but I see another law at work in the members of my body, waging war against the law of my mind and making me a prisoner of the law of sin at work within my members. What a wretched man I am! Who will rescue me from this body of death? Thanks be to God—through Jesus Christ our Lord!
>
> So then, I myself in my mind am a slave to God's law, but in the sinful nature a slave to the law of sin. (Romans 7:21-25)

Earlier in the letter Paul explains that as Christians we have a choice as to which form of control we are going to be under.

> Don't you know that when you offer yourselves to someone to obey him as slaves, you are slaves to the one whom you obey—whether you are slaves to sin, which leads to death, or to obedience, which leads to righteousness? But thanks be to God that, though you used to be slaves to sin, you wholeheartedly obeyed the form of teaching to which you were entrusted. You have been set free from sin and have become slaves to righteousness. (Romans 6:16-18)

Prior to becoming Christians, we were stuck with obeying our sinful nature, which leads to death. Now we have an alternative: We can wholeheartedly give ourselves to God, who sets us free from slavery to sin.

God's Grace and Personal Victory

Enslavement to impurity was a sin that devastated and humbled me prior to becoming a Christian. From the time I was thirteen until I was twenty-three, I masturbated almost every day. Most of those days I was also involved in viewing pornographic magazines, videotapes, or occasionally live strip shows. I always hoped that I would find some degree of fulfillment as I gave myself over to lust. I am convinced that if there were satisfaction and fulfillment to be found in compulsive sexual behavior, I would have found it. And yet, my experience was the same every time that I engaged in this behavior. First came the excitement and hope of finding satisfaction. This was followed by very brief pleasure. The end was always a much longer ache of emptiness and depression. As my habit continued, I found I had to engage in much more extreme behavior to get even the smallest sense of fulfillment.

Becoming a Christian gave me instant and dramatic freedom from the sexual sins that had dominated my life for so long. At the time of this writing, I have been a Christian for about ten years, the first four of which I was totally free of masturbation and viewing pornography. Looking back, I see now that I took a lot of pride in my abstinence. I was very arrogant about this and felt that I just had deeper convictions than most. Brothers would usually only confess their sexual sin to me once or twice and that would be it. I was so harsh, insensitive and judgmental that struggling brothers would usually seek help elsewhere. After about four years as a disciple, I was humbled. I wasn't doing well spiritually. My reactions to life, evangelism and career challenges were ones of hopelessness and frustration. I was not open and did not bring these concerns persistently before God. It was at this time that I learned about the dark side of the Internet, and that with a computer and a modem, a person could conjure up almost any sexual image he might wish to see. The old nature had not gone anywhere! For a period of about ten months, I struggled and often gave in. I viewed pornography and masturbated four or five different times —it was awful!

One of the things that convicted me most in my struggles was the grace and support that the brothers extended me. Alan Holman and Curt Simmons helped me a lot during this time. They were not tolerant of my sin, but they were willing to sit down and talk to me about what was going on in my life. I found their support and guidance in troubling areas of my life a key to becoming victorious in my struggles with impurity. I feel I understand grace a lot better as a result of their help. Further, it is easier now when I am sexually tempted to identify blocked off areas of my soul that are hard to bring before God.

As a counselor, I have found that the sexual struggler needs a healing relationship based on truth and grace. Some of the elements of a healing relationship include: unconditional acceptance of the person (not the sin), an interest in his feelings and a willingness to be open with my own feelings. In my work with others, I have found that the common roots of sexual enslavement usually boil down to three things that most men have difficulty dealing with: stress, anger and sadness. I have had the most success helping people who are enslaved by teaching them to focus on bringing these three emotional states under the control of the Spirit through confession, Bible study and prayer.

Sexually enslaved individuals are often afraid of true closeness and usually keep a tight rein on painful emotions. They become starved for intimacy, but several factors make breaking out of isolation very difficult. First, many such persons tend to have a very strong need for control and/or fear of losing control. Second, surrendering to the full experience of one's feelings involves a partial loss of control.[2] It is my experience with the sexual struggler that unexpressed feelings of sadness and anger are the chief offenders driving the compulsive behavior. Anger and sadness, when full-blown, are probably the least rational and least controllable of our feelings and so are often suppressed. When a man feels the burden of unmet relational needs along with the painful sting of emotions turned inward, he needs an escape. The compulsive sexual cycle can provide this escape. By giving in to improper sexual urges, the sexual struggler strives to release tension, alleviate discomfort and remain in control of his emotions.

Because men typically find it difficult to build relationships, to discuss feelings and to be vulnerable, they are usually more prone to sexual struggles. This is particularly the case for the sexually enslaved. The struggler is bound up with stress, which he bottles up inside by numbing his soul to the perceived threats. As a result of this disconnection, boredom, anxiety and depression set in,

---

[2] *The Anxiety and Phobia Workbook*, by Edmund J. Bourne, Ph.D., provides a great framework for understanding general kinds of compulsive behavior. I think his research on anger and sadness are particularly relevant to sexual addiction.

inhibiting the natural flow of emotions. The man becomes disconnected from his true self. Seeking a way to energize himself and break free from the dull ache of stress, he uses the excitement of sexual behavior to "jump start" his soul with a false intimate connection.[3] The problem is that all of this occurs outside of God's plan and power. The sexual struggler is managing things his own way. As a result, there is no personal growth, no building of character and no increase in faith. The loving discipline of God becomes the enemy, rather than the vehicle for becoming more like Christ. A key to breaking free of sexually compulsive behavior is learning to cope with stress, anger and sadness in a Biblical way.

Controlled by the Spirit

Recently, because I found myself much more tempted with lust than usual, I realized that being controlled by the Spirit includes being personally fruitful in bringing friends to Christ. This is not an optional part of Christianity. I live on the West side of Los Angeles and evangelism seems tough at times. People appear to be richer, busier and more intimidating to me. In my flesh, I tell myself that I am no good at meeting people; it is hard to share my testimony with them; and they probably won't listen anyway. I have had a million excuses for not being faithful to the purpose of the Master. Sexual sin is one of the ways my sinful nature has learned to soothe my soul when I am uncomfortable or unhappy. My apathy was really an effort to block how much of a failure I felt I was as a Christian. By addressing my fears and my lack of love, and by persevering through the loving discipline of God, my temptations have been banished. And a funny thing happened as well: suddenly people seem a lot more approachable, and "rich" West L.A. seems like the most open place on earth!

Overcoming enslavement to sexual sin is much more than simply "not giving in" to sexual temptation. My good friend, James Hamann, always used to tell me that effective Christianity is having a "spiritual offense as well as defense." It involves continually and persistently confessing, repenting of, and praying about every area of my life that is not Christ-like. There is no middle ground. We are either becoming more like Christ or returning to the control of our

[3] *Reparative Therapy of Male Homosexuality*, by Joseph Nicolosi, describes the sexual compulsive behavior of male homosexuals in great detail. I believe his descriptions portray many similarities shared by heterosexual sex addict's lives.

sinful nature (Colossians 3:1-11). I realize that for some people, sexual enslavement is really the outward symptom of deep wounds inflicted on their soul through living in a fallen world. Problems like homosexuality, childhood sexual abuse and life-long depression frequently occur along with sexual enslavement. These problems, and others like them, have deep roots and take time and painstaking effort to dig out. Books, Biblical counseling and the support of others are invaluable for identifying the origin of these struggles. The power to overcome, however, can be found in only one place. Seeking to be controlled by the Spirit through reverent submission to God is the only chance any of us has for defeating our sinful natures. Don't give up! Strive to address the tough areas of your life and bring them persistently before God and others.

18

Disciples, the Internet and Pornography
Declan Joyce

By the time you finish reading this article, another new pornographic Web site will have gone online. As you sleep tonight, another seventy or so will be added. Pornographic Web sites are being added to the untold numbers already online at a rate of 8,000 per month. With so many disciples using the Internet on a regular basis, and the communications revolution making ever deeper invasion into daily life, there is good reason to be concerned. Pornography is an enormously powerful, insidious sin that, if unchecked, has the potential to wreck our faith, our marriages, our children, our lives and our church. And it is freely available to any disciple with a personal computer and phone line.

Easy Access

For many disciples, of course, Internet use presents no particular problem. Pornographic material is there, but they righteously choose to avoid it. For others, however, especially those who have been heavily involved in impurity prior to making a decision to follow Jesus, the temptation to use pornography does not just go away after baptism. Because this sin is among the hardest sins to be open about, however, the true extent of the problem often remains hidden beneath the surface. "Recently, I shared in a church service about some of the problems with pornography I have had," says a thirty-five-year-old disciple in Washington, D.C. "Since that time, I have become a magnet for disciples with similar struggles."

The bewilderingly rapid rise of the new technology has presented disciples with challenges that have simply never existed to such a degree before. Gone are the days when accessing pornography meant slinking guiltily into the neighborhood video store. Pornography is now pumped into our homes twenty-four hours a day. Even those disciples who have made the decision not to have an Internet connection in their homes must still often work in an environment where online access is as basic an office staple as the water cooler or the coffee station. The effect is not unlike a disciple who is recovering from alcohol addiction working a job as a bartender.

"I do not know too many brothers who have not struggled to some extent with Internet pornography," says one prominent leader in the Los Angeles church. "It has undermined marriages, wrecked dating relationships, and made single men weak and enslaved. I think we need to seek radical solutions."

Putting Up a Hedge

What are those solutions? What can you do to protect yourself and/or your family? There are options, but none are fail-safe. Where there is a will, there is a way, and even the most sophisticated filtering services cannot fully screen the volume of material that is thrown at them. The good news is that we do have a fail-safe program, and it is found in the Bible: a willingness to be humble and open about our struggles, to take godly advice, to seek encouragement and inspiration from the Scriptures, and to daily pray for strength and conviction. Without these, any other precaution or strategy is doomed to failure.

On the other hand, part of having conviction is to avail ourselves of what safety measures do exist. The following is a list of some options that may prove useful.

1. Use a filter service. Although not infallible, these do provide some protection. Different kinds are available. Some operate by running the material you access online through a proxy server, which screens out objectionable material. These services charge a monthly fee. One of these, PureISP, is run by members of the International Churches of Christ. PureISP.com is a reseller of the "Rated G" service that was awarded "1999 Best Filtered ISP" (Internet Service Provider) by Best of the Christian Web.

Another option is to purchase software, such as CyberPatrol or Net Nanny, that is stored locally on your computer. The problem with this option is that with pornographic sites being added to the Internet at such a blinding rate, the list of blocked sites must be regularly revised, which is usually done by downloading updates from the software company. This, needless to say, gets expensive. A cheaper option is the internal control software offered by Internet service providers like America Online. For help in setting this up, see *PC Magazine's* article "Fine Tuning the AOL Parental Controls."[1]

A third filtering option is programs such as BizGuard, which are also stored on your computer, but operate by reading the site you are trying to access for profanity. If any is found, the site is blocked. The problem is that some sites don't contain verbal content. In addition, non-pornographic sites may also be blocked, which can get irritating. BizGuard also does not filter many ISPs such as America Online. On the positive side, newer versions of BizGuard include a nondeleteable log of the sites you have visited. As such, it can also be used at home if you are willing to turn yourself in and let your spouse or roommate access this list.

2. *The password method.* When you sign up with an Internet Service Provider, you have the option of setting up a password, which you will then need to access the Internet. Have the password setup done by a spouse or roommate who does not have difficulties with pornography and who can put you online when you need to work or just have a surf party. If they have to leave the house, take yourself offline. This is both humbling and potentially very effective, but again, not fail-safe.

3. *Do without.* Do you really need to be online? For many of us, a Web connection is like a cell phone: We got along quite well without one until everyone and their mother started walking around with a StarTac strapped to their right ear. The Internet is not cheap and can be a major time-waster.

For starters, add up the hours you spend online each week. What dreams could you be pursuing and realizing in that time? How different would your personal ministry be? Above all, if

[1] www.zdnet.com/products/stories/reviews/0,4161,2576030,00.html

having an Internet connection is wrecking your relationship with God, with your wife or with your children, you need to get offline, and you need to do it now. "If your eye offends you...."

If for some reason your career depends on your having Internet access, you should consider approaching your boss or supervisor about installing PureISP or a similar service on your workstation.

Committing to Openness

Above all, it is crucial that you be open about the problems you are having. "My openness has saved me more than anything," says one disciple. "I tried to repent without confessing, and it doesn't work." As with any sin, this is not a battle you can hope to win on your own. And the consequences for losing are, to say the very least, severe.

Anything that is good can be used for evil. The same Internet that can be used to reach millions of people with the message of Jesus can be used to tear lives apart. As disciples, we have committed our lives to be temples of God. Let's keep them clean.

Originally published on the KNN Web site found at www.kingdomnewsnet.org. Used by permission.

19

Understanding the Differences in Men and Women
A Guide Especially for Married Men
Jim Blough

"Men are from Mars, women are from Venus."

–John Gray, Ph.D.

Over the centuries, thousands of books, films, plays, research projects, weekend conferences, backyard conversations and even courtroom proceedings have dealt with the differences between men and women. In recent years, this timeless topic has caught the attention of prominent psychologists and sociologists and now even serves as the focus of a daytime television show. Looking back on our own life experiences, we all remember that exciting stage when we first realized that the opposite sex was not only different, but also interesting and attractive. Truly, it is one of the great marvels of life that "God created man in his own image, in the image of God he created him; male and female he created them" (Genesis 1:27).

Everyone recognizes significant differences between the sexes, but too often these differences become a source of conflict and frustration in marriage, rather than helping to draw us closer together.

If we are ever to build an exciting, powerful relationship with a woman, it is vital that we go beyond mere recognition to actually *understanding* these differences and how they affect us as we interact with one another. Hopefully this chapter will help to stimulate your thoughts toward a deeper understanding and appreciation of the women God has put in your life.

Communication

Communication is one of the greatest joys of marriage, but it can also be one of its biggest challenges. Almost every wife would love for her husband to use more words, be more expressive, provide more detail and take more interest in his own verbal communication. Most men, on the other hand, tend to share a few basic facts and feel that they have accomplished the task of communication. Men do not even notice the details that women feel are essential to truly "capture the moment": *"What was she wearing?" "How are their kids doing?" "How did you feel when...?"*

The key difference between the male and female perspective on communication has to do with its purpose. Men tend to communicate in order to exchange information, but women use communication to cultivate a feeling of intimacy, of being known and understood by another person. Interestingly, the primary cause for infidelity among women is not physical attraction, but rather the development of an emotional attachment with another person through ordinary conversation. In that context, consider this verse:

> Now the serpent was more crafty than any of the wild animals the LORD God had made. He said to the woman, "Did God really say, 'You must not eat from any tree in the garden'?" (Genesis 3:1)

Satan knows that women need to communicate—that is why he chose to engage Eve first through the use of words. He did not send a handsome young man her way, but instead, he approached her through innocent conversation. Not only that, but he asked her a question and waited for her to answer, as if he was actually interested in what she thought and how she felt. And where was Adam while all this was going on? Adam had set his wife up for spiritual disaster by not being available to listen when she needed to talk. *Husbands, if we do not learn to communicate with our wives deeply and often, we leave them open to be seduced by Satan through other relationships.*

One of the things which makes communication challenging for men is that we feel we need to take action on everything our wives tell us. Your wife shares about a problem with the kids or something that went wrong around the house, and you immediately start feeling the pressure to discipline the kids, fix the leaky faucet or solve world hunger. Remember, guys, what our wives really want is to *be heard and understood.* Amazingly, if you can just sit and listen to what she has to say, she will feel much happier and much closer to you when she is done, and you will not have fixed a thing. Just listen to women when they talk to one another. They do not solve each other's problems—they just share how they feel and empathize with one another. Learn to be a great communicator, and you will have a happy wife and a happy home.

Parenting

As we raise our children in the Lord, it does not take long to realize that Mom and Dad have different instinctive responses to parenting situations. Although this can be frustrating, it is actually a gift of God (especially for the children!). Consider these verses from 1 Thessalonians:

> As apostles of Christ we could have been a burden to you, but we were gentle among you, like a mother caring for her little children. (1 Thessalonians 2:6-7)

> For you know that we dealt with each of you as a father deals with his own children, encouraging, comforting and urging you to live lives worthy of God, who calls you into his kingdom and glory. (1 Thessalonians 2:11-12)

We find in these passages that a mother's love is characterized by gentleness, by tender concern and a desire to meet the needs of her children. A father's love, on the other hand, is characterized by encouragement, by urging his children to press forward as far as possible. Typically, Dad shouts "Climb higher!" while Mom calls out "Be careful!"

The inevitable result of these contrasting perspectives on love is that, when children misbehave, Mom and Dad tend to respond differently. Typically (but not always), Dad tends to crack down, take a stand and do battle, while mom is more inclined to talk things through, to try to understand how her children feel and what is going on inside them. Too often, these different responses actually lead to conflict between the parents. Junior bites his baby brother, and suddenly Mom and Dad are arguing with each other!

Whose perspective is right? Consider these verses:

> The Word became flesh and made his dwelling among us. We have seen his glory, the glory of the One and Only, who came from the Father, full of grace and truth. (John 1:14)

> For the law was given through Moses; grace and truth came through Jesus Christ. No one has ever seen God, but God the One and Only, who is at the Father's side, has made him known. (John 1:17-18)

To put it in Biblical terms, Dad usually emphasizes truth, and Mom leans toward grace. If a child is raised in an environment of grace without truth, he will never learn obedience and discipline, and if he grows up experiencing truth without grace, he will struggle to bond and give his heart. What was unique about Jesus is that he combined both grace and truth in a single package. The beauty of God's plan for parenting is that, when Mom and Dad work together as partners, supporting one another as a parenting team, their children will have the proper environment of both grace and truth in which to grow and mature.

Self-Esteem

A fundamental difference between men and women has to do with where we look for self-esteem in our lives. Consider these verses spoken by God to Adam and Eve after they sinned in the garden:

> To the woman he said,
>
> "I will greatly increase your pains in childbearing;
> with pain you will give birth to children.

Your desire will be for your husband,
     and he will rule over you." (Genesis 3:16)

To Adam he said...,

"Cursed is the ground because of you;
     through painful toil you will eat of it
     all the days of your life.
It will produce thorns and thistles for you,
     and you will eat the plants of the field.
By the sweat of your brow
     you will eat your food
until you return to the ground." (Genesis 3:17-19)

As a result of their rebellion against him, God "sentenced" Eve to a life of focusing on family, and he "sentenced" Adam to a life of hard work. It is amazing that after centuries and generations, things have not changed a bit. When men get together, what do they talk about? Work! And when women gather, what do they discuss? Their families! The environment in which we live may have changed over the years, but the basic nature of man and woman remains the same. Women look primarily to their families for their sense of self-worth and meaning in life, and men look primarily to their work responsibilities.

This is a simple but profound point. Men are concerned about performance, women about relationships. This difference can cause conflict in the most unusual of situations. Shortly after Donna and I were married, she needed a new winter coat, so I took her shopping. She found one she seemed to like, so I said, "Let's get it!" (I wanted to buy the coat and get out of there, to cross that item off the day's to-do list.) Donna responded with, "No, now I know it is here and I can come back later if I want to. Let's keep looking."

Why the conflict? We were there for different reasons. I thought the goal was to buy something, to "be productive," to transact business. I had come with wallet open and shopping bag in hand. Donna was there to spend time, to be together, to enjoy the process. If we bought a coat, that was great, but it was not essential. We were together and that was what mattered most to her. For her it was all about relationship, but I was focused on getting something accomplished. She was happy and I was frustrated.

This same dynamic appears in men's and women's sports. If a man misses a shot, everybody shouts at him. If a woman strikes out, all her teammates encourage her with hugs and high-fives. Brothers, if your wife is discouraged, do not expect her to respond the way you do. I usually go for a run or cut the grass when I am feeling a bit low. Having something to do just perks me up. When Donna feels down, though, she probably needs to find a friend and talk, to share what is on her heart and reconnect. That is what makes the difference for her. Remember, women need relationships to feel happy and secure, while we just go off and find something to do.

Strength and Weakness

Related to this discussion on self-esteem is the concept of strength and weakness as it pertains to men and women. Consider this verse from 1 Peter:

> Husbands, in the same way be considerate as you live with your wives, and treat them with respect as the weaker partner and as heirs with you of the gracious gift of life, so that nothing will hinder your prayers. (1 Peter 3:7)

This verse describes women as the "weaker partner." Obviously, this is not a favorite verse with the feminist movement, but what exactly is Peter referring to here? What does it mean that the wife is the weaker partner?

When it comes to dealing with physical pain, most women are tougher than men hands down. The challenges of childbirth, of dealing with hormonal cycles, of frequent illness in the midst of ongoing responsibilities, of laboring tirelessly, caring for family and often working outside the home as well—there is a degree of toughness possessed by women than most men can only dream of. When a man gets sick, the whole world knows. When his wife is ill, she does not even bother to tell him. Physically, women are at least as tough as men.

Women are emotionally tough as well. In a tense discussion between husband and wife, who typically gives up first? It is the man! As men, we often want peace at any price, but our wives are so persistent that they will push and push until matters are truly resolved. If there are challenging relationships with in-laws or other family members, who generally pushes whom to intervene? Even when it comes to disciplining the children, often the wife is more intense than the husband. Women show emotional toughness as well.

So what does the phrase "weaker partner" mean? I believe it means that, because women are in a submissive role and are vulnerable to their husbands, they can be easily hurt. They are tough, but they are also tender. An inconsiderate man can do a great deal of damage to his sensitive wife by thinking that "she's tough, she can handle it." She may take on the neighbors, the relatives and the teachers at school, but she does not want to take on her husband. He has a power over her by virtue of her submissive role to him that can reduce her to tears in a minute and remove all sense of confidence and self-respect with a single harsh word or a cross look.

> **If we are ever to build an exciting, powerful relationship with a woman, it is vital that we go beyond mere recognition to actually understanding these differences and how they affect us as we interact with one another.**

Men, let's never think that we are the tough ones and our wives are weak. This is just not true. It is true, however, that because we are the leaders and they are in a submissive role, we can do a great deal of damage if we are inconsiderate and harsh toward our wives. Not only that, but God will not even listen to our prayers if we are treating them in this way! It is vital that we learn to build up our wives, to show them respect and tenderness as the loving, sensitive companions that God has given us.

Sex and Intimacy

Sex is definitely one of the highlights of the marriage relationship, but it also has the potential to be the most frustrating. Perhaps in no other area of marriage are the differences between husband and wife highlighted in such dramatic fashion. Fortunately, the Bible contains God's perfect wisdom on nearly every topic imaginable, and sex is no exception. The first and most obvious Biblical point about sex is that it should only be enjoyed within the security and commitment of the marriage relationship:

> Marriage should be honored by all, and the marriage bed kept pure, for God will judge the adulterer and all the sexually immoral. (Hebrews 13:4)

The world today does not hold to this standard, the consequences of which are obvious. Unwanted pregnancy, abortion, and millions of children raised in dysfunctional family situations all result from this frivolous, casual attitude toward sex. The interesting thing to note, though, is that this attitude is driven much more by men than women. What most women want is a committed, loving relationship, and studies have shown that the majority of women are less able to respond sexually to their partners in the absence of commitment and love. In fact, happily married conservative Christian women have been shown to be one of the most sexually responsive groups in the entire American population!

This highlights a crucial difference in the attitude of men and women toward sex. Women need emotional closeness and intimacy to enjoy sex, and men need sex to enjoy emotional closeness and intimacy. Most men feel closer to their partners after sex, but women need to feel close before sex if they are to enjoy it.

God's wisdom can be clearly seen here, for in order to have a mutually satisfying sexual relationship, both husband and wife must give of themselves to meet their partner's needs. Consequently, sex becomes an act of giving and self-sacrifice rather than an act of making demands and self-gratification. Most men are too eager to consummate the act and do not take enough time to encourage their wives verbally and patiently. Consider these words from the Song of Songs:

> *Lover*
> I liken you, my darling, to a mare
>   harnessed to one of the chariots of Pharaoh.
> Your cheeks are beautiful with earrings,
>   your neck with strings of jewels.

We will make you earrings of gold,
　　studded with silver. (Song 1:9-11)

These are the very first words spoken by the Lover to his Beloved in this classic Biblical treatment of sexual love. See how he identifies specific qualities to praise in his beloved, rather than the "You're awesome, honey!" too often spoken by the lazy-minded husband who knows that he *should* build up his wife, but doesn't want to take the time to think of something meaningful to say. The Lover in this passage likens his wife to a mare, spirited, strong and beautiful, drawing the chariot of Pharaoh through the streets.

The Lover encourages his partner by talking about her beauty, and once again he is specific and expressive in his words. Too often we introduce our spouses with the trite phrase "Here is my beautiful wife," but we never take the time to tell her exactly which parts of her we find beautiful, and how we feel about her beauty. Specific, verbal encouragement is a powerful tool to build the emotional intimacy and closeness a woman needs to respond sexually to her partner.

Finally, note that the Lover gives gifts to his Beloved. Even though she already has a pair of earrings, he wants to give her more. What's wrong with the earrings she already has? That's not the point—his attentiveness to her, his verbal encouragement and descriptions of her beauty and his desire to shower her with gifts she doesn't even need—all these combine to create the emotional intimacy she needs and craves. Remember, women need to feel emotionally close if they are to respond sexually to their husbands.

Why All the Differences?

Having discussed several important differences between men and women, the question must be raised, "Why did God create all these differences?" Wouldn't it have been easier if we were not so different—then we could be unified without so much conflict and arguing. It is so easy to look at the differences in my wife and think that if she were only more like me, life would be so much easier. As Professor Henry Higgins put it in *My Fair Lady*, "Why can't a woman be like a man?" Can you relate? These differences between us can become a sore point, a source of conflict, of disappointment and ultimately even of separation or divorce.

The Bible teaches a simple but profound point: Our strengths divide us, but our weaknesses unite us. If we feel that we are always right and our partner is always wrong, we will continually be frustrated and focused on the areas that she needs to change. The problem here, though, is a lack of humility on our part. Rather than feeling that I am right, if I can have the attitude of weakness in approaching the marriage relationship, that "I need you because you make up for my shortcomings," then the frustration quickly dissolves into appreciation. Consider this passage as it relates to marriage:

> To keep me from becoming conceited because of these sur-passingly great revelations, there was given me a thorn in my flesh, a messenger of Satan, to torment me. Three times I pleaded with the Lord to take it away from me. But he said to me, "My grace is sufficient for you, for my power is made perfect in weakness." Therefore I will boast all the more gladly about my weaknesses, so that Christ's power may rest on me. That is why, for Christ's sake, I delight in weaknesses, in insults, in hardships, in persecutions, in difficulties. For when I am weak, then I am strong. (2 Corinthians 12:7-10)

One woman who read this in the editing process wondered if I was comparing women to thorns in the flesh! In no way! I am just using the passage to show how God works in my weaknesses. Let me give an example. I am a hard-working, productive person by nature. I may be more productive than my wife, but if I were the only parent in our family, our children would be neurotic, paranoid workaholics who were always afraid of failing. I need my wife's fun-loving spirit and playful attitude to help my children (and myself!) to feel happy and secure in life, and to not always be worrying about the things that are not getting done. Rather than looking at my productivity and drive as a great strength, I actually see it as a weakness, as an area where my wife can help me to be more what God wants me to be. I also need my wife to help me overcome my shallowness in communication, my selfishness in sex, my harshness in parenting and my focus on productivity.

In his wisdom, when God created man in his image, he created us "both male and female." One of us does not present the complete picture of God, but together, as partners helping to compensate for one another's weaknesses, we can enjoy an incredible intimacy, create a wonderful environment in which our children can grow and thrive, and become more and more like Christ in the process. Let's resolve that our differences will no longer push us apart, but that they will draw us closer and closer together as we grow in Christ.

20

How to Renew Your Marriage

Tracy Larr

Twenty years ago, at the age of eighteen, my wife, Phyllis, and I were married. We were young and in love, yet had no idea what we were getting into. We had dated since we were sixteen (she was my first "car" date) and knew we wanted to be together for the rest of our lives, but we had no concept of the challenges and hardships we would face along the way.

Nine years into our relationship, our marriage looked good on the outside, but was secretly scarred by sexual immorality, adultery, bitter fits of rage and anger, threats of divorce and a host of deceit to cover it all up. We needed help, and we needed it in the worst way. We decided to go through what would become both the most emotionally challenging and yet emotionally fulfilling experience of our lives. We underwent a "marriage reconstruction" or a "marriage renewal." Whatever you call it, we radically dealt with all the sin in our relationship and began to rebuild our marriage according to God's will and purpose.

I am assuming that if you choose to read this chapter, you feel that your marriage needs renewal on some level. Maybe it's gone "flat" over the years and has lost some of its pep. Perhaps age, children, bills and life in general have sidetracked you from that fresh young love that first characterized your relationship. Or perhaps, like my marriage, it is as simple as allowing sin to wreak havoc on your life and threaten to totally destroy the one relationship on earth you cherish the most. Whatever your situation is, there is hope. Your marriage can be changed and renewed to the young, idealistic (though wiser) love you had at first.

Remembering the Love You Had at First

In Revelation 2:4-5 Jesus called the church in Ephesus to "remember the height from which you have fallen. Repent and do the things you did at first." Their primary problem was that they had forsaken their "first love." Their relationship with God had deteriorated into a system of actions and works that were without heart and emotion. They did the right things, but with the wrong motivation. This happened in my relationship with my wife. How about you?

The primary key to renewing my marriage, and keeping it new, is to remember how much I love my wife, Phyllis. I say it is primary because it gives me the motivation to deal with whatever problems and challenges we face, regardless of how difficult they may be.

I constantly remind myself of why I fell in love with Phyllis, how I felt in those early teen years, what it was about Phyllis that attracted me to her and to her alone. Even when I would break up with her and date someone else, something always brought me back to Phyllis. This is the heart and motivation I must always stay in touch with.

After first meeting Phyllis, I went home that night and told my mother that I had met the girl I was going to marry. We dated off and on for the next three years until we got married. We built a lot of good memories during that time which I treasure in my heart and build on, even today.

Take some time to write out a list of all the things that first attracted you to your wife. Write out all the things that caused you to fall in love with her the first time. Keeping these memories fresh in your heart is vital to keeping your marriage fresh.

Loving Teamwork

The second step in renewing your marriage is to commit to working together as a team. She is my partner; we are a team, a pair, a couple. We chose each other for life. In Genesis 2:24, God uses the

Hebrew word *dabaq* ("be united") to describe the relationship between a husband and his wife. According to *Strong's*, the definition of this word is: "*cling* or *adhere*; figurative to *catch* by pursuit: abide fast, cleave (fast together), follow close (hard after), be joined (together), keep (fast), overtake, pursue hard, stick, take." It is very important for me to remember these phrases in my marriage. No matter what is going on between Phyllis and me, I must remember that she is my partner, not my enemy. She is the one I want to "follow close (hard after)." She is the one I chose to "stick" to. I may not always know what problems Phyllis and I may face or who is to blame, but I do know that Phyllis is not an enemy to be defeated, dominated or destroyed. She and I are on the same team. We both want the same thing.

I have often made the mistake of thinking that Phyllis and I were in competition for what each of us wants, that our personal desires and needs were somehow diametrically opposed, and that I could not be happy if she got her way and visa versa. Yet this is the woman I decided years ago I could not be happy without—how twisted my thinking can be! I must dig deep into my heart and hold onto what I truly want and desire: a great marriage with my wife.

We all know that ministries and discipleship partners are bound to change with time. We also have seen how jobs and co-workers can change overnight. Even our children will someday move out of the house to begin their own lives. There is only one person on this planet that I intend to grow old and gray with, one person that I foresee myself waking up next to every morning for the next thirty-five to forty years: my wife, Phyllis. Therefore, this is the one relationship that I absolutely insist must be great. We are a team for life—and life is too long to live any other way.

Dealing with Sin

If you have the first two steps down, then you are ready for the third step: radically dealing with all the sin in your relationship—all the sin, both past and present. This is the most difficult part of renewing your marriage. After dating for so long without Jesus as Lord of our lives, Phyllis and I had ample opportunity to build up quite a history of sin and pain. Although we were not disciples, we were very religious and knew what God's expectations were for our relationship. In spite of this, our dating relationship became characterized by selfishness and immorality.

At first it was difficult to see how these sins that were "so long ago" could still be affecting our marriage. We could not see how they had subtly built a foundation of mistrust, suspicion and regret between us. The implication was that if we could not trust each other to be righteous before our wedding, how could we trust each other after? The sin that so enslaved me as a teen continued to haunt me, and later it almost cost me my marriage.

After about five years of a very angry and volatile marriage, I again surrendered to my sinful, selfish nature and became involved with a married woman. I stopped the relationship after a few weeks and never told anyone. Soon after, Phyllis and I moved to Boston to pursue our relationship with God. It was not until a few years later that I was open with Phyllis about my sin of adultery. I will never forget the pain and hurt in her eyes.

It was hard to see how that sin had driven a wedge between Phyllis and me, especially when she knew nothing about it. But all sin destroys—even secret sin. I was not free to love her as she needed or deserved. Our marriage was held prisoner by my past and my fear of openness. It was not until I got brutally honest with Phyllis that our marriage could really bloom into the relationship that God wanted.

Let me offer a word of caution here: *Do not try this on your own!* I do not even want to think about what would have happened if I had tried to tell Phyllis this news on my own. I thank God for Terry and Sue Folker who were there to help us through a very rough time. If you have sin in your life that you need to be open about, get the help and support of godly men and women who will be there for you and your wife so that Satan does not turn what should be a great victory into a horrible defeat. It is imperative that you get the sin out, but do it wisely.

Forgiving and Forgetting

Colossians 3:13 says, "Bear with each other and forgive whatever grievances you may have against one another. Forgive as the Lord forgave you." After I was open with my sin, Phyllis forgave me, and we were free to go about the business of rebuilding our marriage. It was not until several months later that we realized just how far off base we were. While I had been open with my sin, we had not really dealt with the hurt and pain that was in our relationship.

Again, with the help of godly men and women, we were able to talk through *all* the hurts and disappointments in our marriage. It was so freeing to specifically and verbally apologize for all the sin we could remember from our dating life until that very day and to affirm each time our forgiveness to each other.

There is such power in the two phrases, "I am so sorry for [fill in the blank]. Will you forgive me?" and "Yes, I forgive you." It was very important that we verbalize our regret and our forgiveness for everything. We left no room for Satan to bring things back up. After you have "cleaned the slate," never forget these two phrases. I find I have to use them—especially the first one—quite often.

I pray that God can use my experiences and the lessons he has taught me to both encourage and help you to keep your marriage fresh and exciting.

21

Raising Righteous Daughters

Mike Fontenot

In one of the most dramatic prophetic scenes in the Old Testament, the prophet Nathan approaches King David to inform him about an injustice amongst his people. A rich, unjust farmer has taken a poor farmer's only lamb to serve to his guests. Though he had many lambs of his own, he takes the poor farmer's only beloved ewe lamb. Their relationship is described like this: "It shared his food, drank from his cup and even slept in his arms. It was like a daughter to him" (2 Samuel 12:3b). It was not really about a ewe lamb at all, but about David's injustice against Uriah by taking his only wife in adultery. But the anecdote was meant to tug on the heartstrings. *It was like a daughter!* God uses this same image to describe his people as the "Daughter of Zion" and "the apple of God's eye." As a father of three daughters, my emotions are aroused by what Nathan said because naturally, fathers feel deeply about their daughters. We are easily moved by popular songs that remind us of our paternal feelings. Even the less emotional of us find ourselves brushing back the tears thinking about our daughters growing up and remembering those "butterfly kisses."

How can we raise our daughters to be faithful, spiritual women? What Biblical insights can help us with this awesome task? Let's look at several principles that I have used in raising my daughters.

Word-Centered Homes

"The days are coming," declares the Sovereign LORD,
    "when I will send a famine through the land—
not a famine of food or a thirst for water,
    but a famine of hearing the words of the LORD.
Men will stagger from sea to sea
    and wander from north to east,
searching for the word of the LORD,
    but they will not find it.

"In that day

    "the lovely young women and strong young men
        will faint because of thirst." (Amos 8:11-13)

A common visitor's observation attending one of our services is often, "It is so good to see so many young people here. Usually the churches I visit are filled with older people." Now I believe that there may be a reason for that, which is tied to Amos' prophecy. There are no "lovely young women and strong young men" because there is a famine and absence of the word of God preached and lived out in many churches. Now if this principle is true of the church, it is true of the home as well. Are our homes Word centered? Is it taught there? Are the Scriptures talked about at our tables, as we travel, when we work in our yards or during sporting events? Are the Scriptures brought in as daily and practical answers to our problems, solutions to our needs and resolutions of the dramas of life?

Having a family devotional was a regular part of our family life each week while raising our kids. At that time there was always a lesson and always an application to our lives of the Biblical principles we had chosen to live out as Christians. They included confession time and discipling time—with no one being exempt. They were not heavy times, but they were direct and fun. We had lots of singing and always prayer and the Word. We must have a Word-centered home in order to raise "lovely young women" and to receive the blessing described in Psalm 144:12 (NLT):

> May our sons flourish in their youth
>> like well-nurtured plants.
> May our daughters be like graceful pillars,
>> carved to beautify a palace.

Our daughters will not be graceful pillars unless they have been shaped by God's hand through his Scriptures.

Strong, Spiritual Fathers

Some examples in the Bible are negative examples teaching fathers what not to do in raising our daughters. I can think of no worse example than Lot (Genesis 19). The story of Lot started going downhill when he selfishly chose the best land as he separated from his uncle, Abraham. The land he chose reminded him of Egypt, which began his slow drift away from God, ending up with him sitting in the gateway (a metaphor of leadership) of the city of Sodom.

The evil of Sodom and Gomorrah had overstretched God's mercy, and destruction was imminent. After much supplication from Abraham, two angels are sent looking for at least ten righteous people. Abraham I'm sure hoped that at least six of the righteous would be his relatives: Lot, his wife, his two daughters and their fiancés. When the angels arrived, Lot pleaded with them to come under his roof for protection against the immoral population. As the men of Sodom surrounded his house, wanting to abuse the two angels, Lot offers them his virgin daughters to abuse as a substitute for the men:

> "Please, my brothers," he begged, "don't do such a wicked thing. Look—I have two virgin daughters. Do with them as you wish, but leave these men alone, for they are under my protection." (Genesis 19:7-8)

This is a pathetically low point in the Bible. The incident continued to decline as Lot was laughed at by his future sons-in-law as he pleaded with them to escape the approaching destruction. I wonder what they thought of his spiritual leadership after having seen him offer their fiancées to the crowd? They are finally dragged out of Sodom by God's grace.

Lot's wife looked back instead of following her husband and was turned to salt, and Lot and his daughters ended up hiding in a cave in the mountains. The two daughters were without their fiancés and worried about preserving the family, so they got him drunk on consecutive nights in order to sleep with him. Their descendants became the forefathers of both the Moabites and Ammonites, the stumbling blocks for Israel as they entered the promised land. It is a long, sad story, but it is filled with illustrations about how not to father daughters. Strong, spiritual, fatherly leadership is absent and the horrifying result is obvious.

Decision Making

What are some of the lessons from Lot's story? Let me tell you several that have helped me. First, always make family decisions that are best for your daughters by asking many questions, like the following: Why did Lot and his family move to this city? What possible explanation was there for putting his family at such a perilous risk? Was it for a job, or did he like the climate or culture? Who are these two men who are engaged to his daughters? We do not just need to make good decisions—we need to make the *best possible* decisions. Personally, I decided to never make any decisions that would ever endanger my daughters' righteousness. This had mostly to do with me being righteous, not just our location. It is not just Sodom but Lot's own spiritual condition, his own selfishness, which is the worse influence on his family.

Leading Means Leading

Next, always lead your family; do not just agree with them. At times Lot is blown around by other forces. He is carried along sometimes by other powers (Abraham had to rescue him earlier). Today, there are winds and waves of opinion, both outside and inside the church, that we feel obliged to drift with—even when we do not necessarily agree. Leadership involves setting a great personal example and making decisions that you think are best, of course always by seeking advice, thus increasing your chances for success (Proverbs 19:20).

Our family has lived in three different countries while serving in the ministry. On every occasion, my family was willing to follow my lead because they believed that I was putting God and them above my own desires. The possible consequences of not choosing to do the best thing for God were always in the forefront of my mind. I had to ask myself how they would ever learn what it means to be a disciple if I wasn't willing to be a disciple myself. They did not look back whenever we moved (at least not for long) because they trusted my leadership. We moved to Australia when the girls were young, and we prayerfully, faithfully and purposefully converted families who had daughters that were the same age as ours. These girls became our girls' best friends. Maybe you don't think you can do that, but you *can* make decisions that will allow your children to be raised in a place where faith is possible. It is not just about location, but about settling for nothing less than the best for them.

Family over Ambition

The story of Jephthah, who lived in the time of the Judges, is another illustration of what not to do. His six-year rise to power from being the outcast son of a prostitute to a judge leading Israel is outlined in Judges 10-12. Because of his past expulsion due to his illegitimacy, he was very careful in making sure that Israel would really let him lead in a permanent way. In Judges 11:9 Jephthah answered them, "Suppose you take me back to fight the Ammonites and the LORD gives them to me—will I really be your head?" His insecurity cries out in his response. In the midst of the ensuing battle, Jephthah is so driven by his desire to win and lead that he makes a terrible vow to God (Judges 11:30-31). If he could only win, he promised God that whatever would come out of the door of his house, he would sacrifice it as a burnt offering. So, returning from his victory, we see the result of his blind ambition:

> When Jephthah returned to his home in Mizpah, who should come out to meet him but his daughter, dancing to the sound of tambourines! She was an only child. Except for her he had neither son nor daughter. (Judges 11:34)

Why did he make such a vow? What was he expecting to come out of his doorway at home? Did he live with the livestock? What was his motive? I believe his own insecurity and ambition to lead made him willing to do anything to get that position and keep it. What a price to pay for leadership! It is not worth the life of your daughter.

Today, we are still tempted to sacrifice our daughters for leadership. We need to be so careful, lest in our zeal to do or get something, we compromise God's will and desire for our lives. Jephthah totally misunderstood God. God wanted him to be righteous and to deliver his people—he had no desire for him to make such a detestable vow. Be desirous to do great things for God, but understand how great a thing it is to God to raise faithful children.

Raise Givers, not Takers

"The leech has two daughters.
   'Give! Give!' they cry." (Proverbs 30:15)

The meaning of the above proverb seems plain enough. On several occasions while walking through a rain forest, I have found leeches attached to my legs. On other occasions I never knew they were there. Later, however, I would discover blood in my sock because the leech had had its fill and dropped off, having left an anticoagulant where it was attached which kept the blood flowing. They suck until they are full, then drop off.

Why are daughters described as leeches? Do girls like to shop, to go to the mall, a bit more than boys? I suppose so. "Give! Give!" If they are constantly indulged, they can be described as leeches. Are you raising leeches or givers?

Of course we don't want our daughters to be like that. We want just the opposite from them. We want them to be givers, those who take care of others, rather than those who use others for their own indulgences. How do we get them there?

Saying 'No'

There are several things I have learned to do. First, learn to say "No!" I know it sounds like such a little thing, but you are not depriving them of a proper upbringing if they can't have the name brand clothes or do what "all" their classmates do.

Gratitude

Second, teach them to be grateful for what they do have. Whether it is much or little, it doesn't matter. They need to be grateful to you and to God for what they have. They need to learn to say "Thank you" for the opportunity to eat out, go to the movies, take a vacation or get a new pair of sneakers.

Serving

Third, they need to learn to serve whenever possible. Every guest needs to be served, not ignored. Friendliness and warmth need to be given to those who come into contact with us. Being involved in the ministry staff meant that our home had a steady stream of visitors, many coming for the first time. It was crucial to make our outreach a family project. My daughters might not be the ones studying the Bible with them, but their friendliness and service were often key in showing our sincerity to those who did study. It is difficult to distrust a loving family. Our family was geared to saving the lost and caring for people. Now that they have all left the home, being either married or on-campus students, they have continued to be caregivers rather than takers.

Always Desire the Best for Them

One of my biggest heroes in the Old Testament has always been Caleb. Imprinted on my mind is that great statement he made about being as strong at eighty-five as he was when he was forty. I am a long way from eighty-five but definitely over forty, and I most definitely dream of keeping my strength and passion for God. Even in his old age, he wanted his daughter to get hooked up with a strong, spiritual man, so he gives the test in Judges 1:12-13:

> And Caleb said, "I will give my daughter Acsah in marriage to the man who attacks and captures Kiriath Sepher." Othniel son of Kenaz, Caleb's younger brother, took it; so Caleb gave his daughter Acsah to him in marriage.

Othniel later became Israel's first judge. Though his judgeship is mentioned only briefly, there was peace in the land for forty years, until Othniel died. This is the kind of guy whom I want to marry one of my daughters!

Who our daughters marry is a huge decision in terms of their future spirituality and happiness. When the relationship is close between a father and a daughter, she is very interested in whether

her father approves or disapproves. Our oldest daughter was married last August to my first son-in-law, Forest. They are both serving on the ministry staff, and I am so proud of them. It is an answer to many prayers. Every prayer for them and with them each night growing up included a prayer for a strong, spiritual husband in their futures—and it is still a prayer for the other two!

Ultimately, "the best" for our daughters always involved their spiritual lives. We spurred them on academically and athletically, but the greatest spurring was always concerning their spiritual lives. How were their relationships? Were they being evangelistic? Were they caring for others? Church activities were always a priority. If that meant sacrifice, then they learned that following God involved sacrifice, even for them.

Above All

All of my children at this moment, by God's grace, are doing great spiritually. Here are some simple charges. Make sure that you are a deeply spiritual man. Make sure that you are abundantly affectionate with your daughters. This safeguards them from looking for it from other men because most young girls want closeness to a man, not sex. Be sure you are providing this closeness and affection, even when they get more uncomfortable with it as they mature. Be strong and full of fun, spurring your daughters on to new experiences and challenges. Be that anchor for their souls as they travel out and make a life for themselves, knowing you will always be there, trusting and serving God. Proverbs 17:6 says, "Parents are the pride of their children." Be a hero to your daughters and an upward call!

22

Friendship with Your Son
Jaime De Anda, Ph.D.

And a voice from heaven said, "This is my Son, whom I love;
with him I am well pleased."

Matthew 3:17

As I write this, the newspaper headlines and television reports are
bringing home the horrible news: another disturbed teenager
has opened fire at a suburban high school. More young lives have
been lost to the madness that has infected our society. These are difficult times for America's (and the world's) youth. Too many of our
young people are being raised in a moral and spiritual void, without
any guidance other than what they see on television and in the
movies. But I believe that as Christians, we can make a difference,
not only in the lives and souls of our children, but in society as well.

I am the proud father of four boys and one girl. At the time of
writing, Rubén is a junior at UCLA, Bianca is a freshman at Santa
Monica College, Darren is a sophomore in high school, Eric is in sixth
grade, and DJ is in first grade. They are all very unique individuals,
and parenting each one has been a unique, rewarding experience.

I will share mostly about my oldest, Rubén, because it was with
him that I learned most of my lessons as a father. Today I see this
twenty-one-year-old young man, and although I am very proud of

him as my son, I am also very grateful to see him as a friend. This chapter is about the building of that friendship.

Many of us would like a simple to-do list that guarantees instant success in building a friendship, in the same way that many companies sell you a system for instantly building up your business. However, the relationship between you and your son is not a business; it needs to be an evolving friendship. You need to grow together, learn together and mold each other. It will take hard work, but someday…you will look upon that young man, and you will realize that he is not only your son, he has become your friend.

Connection

It was late at night. Rubén was crying in his crib. My wife Mimi and I had agreed to take turns getting up, and it was Dad's turn to check in on the baby. Drowsily, and with some annoyance, I got out of bed to see what Rubén was fussing about. The crib was next to our bed in our one-bedroom apartment. I did not turn on the lights; there was some moonlight filtering through the window. As I approached the crib, Rubén quieted down some. I bent over and found myself looking, in the dim light, at the brightest pair of eyes and the widest smile. His arms went up for me to pick him up. It was as if he was saying, "Let's play!"

As I picked him up, something clicked in my heart, some unknown feeling gelled within me: a mysterious, inexplicable bond was forged between this small being and me. We had connected. This child and I were united for life.

The truth is that our best friends are usually those who were basically "thrown" into our lives at particular moments. Something happened. We hit it off. We bonded. Something clicked between us. We cannot explain what it was. My friendship with Rubén began at that magical moment in the shadows of our room, as I held his little body close to me.

If we are to have great friendships with our sons, this connection must happen. You may have missed it because the worries of life and your harried schedule stole this moment from you. Or perhaps it did happen, but you have forgotten. Your first step is to pray for God to restore this connection.

Conviction

Over the childhood years, God took Rubén and me through many experiences that forged and strengthened our friendship. Oh, there was the usual stuff that dads and sons do: youth sports, school activities, movies, etc. There were also colds and bruises and disappointments. But there was more: There was church! God's kingdom provided a background for everything we did and thought. Every experience, every moment, was cherished because I knew by faith that everything that happened was an expression of God's dynamic presence in our lives. And I knew that, because of this, my relationship with my son was meant to fit into a greater scheme, that its purpose went beyond producing a happy household. This belief strengthened my resolve to work on my relationship with Rubén. It added the power of conviction to the connection that already existed between us.

One of the main ingredients of our developing relationship was for me to teach him about God. As he grew, Mimi and I prayed with him, we taught him church songs, we read scriptures and taught him the great stories from the Bible. I always tried to figure out what was going on inside my son's little head. So, one day we asked five-year-old Rubén to draw a picture of God. He drew a big, amorphous "thing" with a smile on it. We asked him what it was, and he explained, "It's a big rock!" In his own way, he understood one key concept, one foundational value that many children are missing today: There *can* be stability, there *can* be security, there *is* a source of strength in this life, and it is God.

This strength, this stability, this security became a foundation for our family. No matter what challenges we faced, no matter that we would sin and even hurt each other's feelings, we had the constant presence of our Father, always there to love us, hold us and take care of us. This was the context of my relationship with Rubén and my other children. They *knew* that Dad was not perfect, that he could "mess up." But they did not get insecure or destabilized because they knew that God was in control.

Culture

Every family has its own culture. Unfortunately, not many families decide and plan to forge a specific culture in their homes. The result is that such families allow the world's values to influence and mold their relationships, their decisions and their expectations. We decided that the De Anda household would be built on Christ, on values and traditions that would strengthen us, motivate us and build our characters. Although I cannot say that we have achieved this goal fully, I know that God has blessed us and has more than made up for what has been lacking.

Being Hispanics, obviously our household culture was very Latin. So, even before we became Christians, our expectation was for the family to be close-knit forever. And a lot of the things that made our lives fun had to do with elements of our background: the foods, the music and our conversations (in a louder-than-average tone of voice and in not-too-orderly, overlapping style).

To this cultural framework we added our own particular traditions: the Saturday Pancake Breakfast, the Christmas Tree Decorating Evening, the Bedtime Story and Prayer Time, the Family Time, and the Spring Break vacation. These and other elements of our family culture provided fun and great memories to mark the time in the development of our relationships.

However, I want to focus here on one significant aspect: outside influences. When children reach the teen years, their peers and friends become a powerful influence in their lives. Sometimes parents feel that they have to compete with their sons' friends for respect and attention. As a father, I knew that if I wanted to have a strong friendship with my son, I would need help. That help came from church!

Peers

Over the years, I have surrounded our family with other families from the church: parents and children who live by the same principles as we do. Rubén's best friends were always from the church. When they all became teens, they reinforced in each other the values that they had learned growing up.

Role Models

Teenagers tend to perceive their parents as "not being with it," "out of touch" or "not cool." They may end up dismissing our values together with our tastes and preferences. I tried to find fine young men in the church, college students or young single brothers, who would be his "older" friends. These brothers served as role models. They represented a midpoint in age between my son and me. They also lived by the same values and principles that I believed in, so their friendships with my son reinforced these values because he saw them being lived out by these young men whom he admired.

Trends

Are you always critical of your son's clothes or the music he likes? Teenagers sometimes feel that their parents do not really like them. I have kept an open mind and stayed in touch with what is happening in our pop culture: music, movies, fashions, colloquialisms. I do not embrace everything that is out there, but I am able to discuss with my children the merits and flaws of various cultural influences. And they have respected that. They tend to listen to my advice as to what movies not to watch, what music not to listen to, and what fashions not to pursue. They do not see me as a censor, but as an involved friend who wants to teach them how to make good choices. And in learning how to hold onto the values they have been taught, they learn to make solid decisions, and so their character is built.

I have tried to be sensitive to their needs and concerns and to the pressures they feel. I am not just trying to be "relatable"; some parents look clownish in their attempts to relate to their teenagers. I want to know what my children are experiencing out there, so I can guide them and help them. I want them to know that I care about them, that I love them and that I *like* them.

Conversion

Perhaps no experience is as rewarding to a Christian parent as the baptism of his children. Our journey into this phase began, obviously, when we became Christians. A key turning point happened during a Saturday morning breakfast at one of our favorite restaurants. Rubén, thirteen, had just come back from a youth retreat in California, and he was eagerly anticipating this breakfast because he wanted to "have a talk." After sharing about his experiences at the retreat, he said something that I will never forget: "Dad, I want to tell you *everything*."

My son felt that I was approachable; he saw me as someone with whom he could share his inmost thoughts, his fears, his concerns and his temptations. This trust, this bond of friendship, this spirit of openness, is missing in many father-son relationships. As he went through his passage into discipleship, although I did not do the Bible studies with him, we were able to talk about what was going on in his mind as he dealt with his challenges. The night of his baptism was as memorable as that night, years before, when we first "connected."

Continuity

Rubén is currently a ministry intern for the Los Angeles church, where he has helped lead one of the church's teen ministry groups for two years. It is extremely interesting to talk to him about his experience; I find myself learning from him! He tells me about some of the Bible studies they do with the teens and about how they help them to deal with issues in their lives. It has been humbling to learn what mistakes I made as a father, and how I can better help my three sons who still live at home as they go through their teen years.

Recently, I asked Rubén about children who have grown up in the church but do not want to become disciples of Christ. I am not talking about the thirteen-year-old who is too immature to make such a commitment; I am talking about the sixteen- or seventeen-year-old who values his high school friends more than the church. I asked Rubén why that was not such a major hurdle for him. His response was, "They don't want to be like their dads. I wanted to be like you." A father can probably not receive a greater compliment than this, that his children want to imitate his example.

Many of you have small children at home. God has given you a great opportunity to build a great friendship with your son. Do not waste any chance! Enjoy each moment and each day as you see your son grow up into manhood.

Some of you have become Christians more recently, and you did not have the opportunity of raising your son in the kingdom of God. You may feel that what I have written here does not apply to you, that you cannot recapture that connection with your son or build a great friendship anymore. Please let me remind you of the De Andas' family scripture, Psalm 118:1, "Give thanks to the LORD, for he is *good*; his love endures *forever*" (emphasis added). God *is* good. There is no limit to what God's love can accomplish.

You may feel estranged from your teenage son. You may be physically apart from your son due to a separation or divorce. Or maybe he is already grown up and living on his own, perhaps already raising his own family. Reach out to him. Pray for God to help you connect! Strengthen your convictions! Rebuild the culture of your household around Christ and his church! Conversion is not the ultimate goal, but a continued friendship, until you stand before God and can say with the prophet Isaiah:

> Here am I, and the children the LORD has given me. We are signs and symbols in Israel from the LORD Almighty, who dwells on Mount Zion. (Isaiah 8:18)

23

Honoring Father and Mother
A New Perspective for Adult Men
Mike Hammonds

'Honor your father and mother—which is the first command-ment with a promise" (Ephesians 6:2). I suspected that there was more to this verse than I understood. In fact, as I read on, "that it may go well with you and that you may enjoy long life on the earth," I felt that I should probably get familiar with wellness and long life. Because of the ways in which fifty-three years had shaped me, I had much fear about where this verse might take me. However I trusted God enough to know that I would be safe. As I delved into it and its context, I was reminded again that God really has given us "everything we need for life and godliness through our knowledge of him who called us by his own glory and goodness" (2 Peter 1:3).

The Promise Is Wellness

"Honor" in Greek language (*tima*) means to show a careful regard, dignity and consideration toward; to treat graciously and visit with marks of favor. I thought I had always done this toward my father and mother. But I wanted to find out if this were actually true. As I evaluated my life, I knew that wellness was not present in certain areas, as evidenced by my "low-level grade" of anger, my desire to be respected and accepted, and my lack of openness and vulnerability. I also had some recurrent feelings whenever I went home. I always felt, to some degree, a lack of respect and acceptance from my father. What to do? Study this thing out, I supposed.

Ephesians 6:3 literally says in the Greek language, "that wellness thine come to pass to be long duration upon life." (You may have to read that again.) This sounds like God wants wellness to be something in my life that would last. Let me share with you how I have begun to find this lasting wellness.

Beginning with Fathers

The plan from God is for the "fathers" to not exasperate (*me parorgizete* in Greek: to provoke to anger or irritate) but to train (*paideia* in Greek: education, training up, nurture of children; some say it even means, specific and individualized child training) and instruct in the Lord (*nouthesia* in Greek: to admonish, put sense into; implies a change is needed; discipling the heart) their children. Colossians 3:21 says, "Do not embitter" (*me erethizete* in Greek: to provoke, exasperate, irritate, incite) or they will become discouraged (*me athumosin* in Greek: to lose heart, to despond). The role of the father is clear in God's instruction. It is the role immediately following the promise of wellness. In fact, the role of the father is to honor his own father and mother so that his wellness is visited upon his children. I believe that it is from the father's wellness that his own children will honor him and their mother. If we are not resolved about honoring our own parents, then we can hardly pass wellness on to our children.

I must understand God's directive. When I was a child, my father was to consider me for who I was. Based on who I was, he was to child train me and put sense into my life in the Lord. The reality is that my father did not do this. He did what was done to him, or he did what he thought he should do, or he did very little. The result was exasperation, anger and hope lost on my part. My father was home every night; he provided for the material needs of his family; he was at all the athletic events; he thought he was doing all he should and could; however, I strove in vain to gain his acceptance and respect. So, what is wrong here? For who I was, as God made me, what I needed was for him to put his arm around me and say, "I am proud of you"; "you are doing a good job"; "you are my special boy"; "you are my prince"; and "I am here for you." This is just the way that God made me.

Interestingly enough, I spent many years trying to gain affirmation from my father in almost every circumstance I encountered. I finally realized that in one sense, I never left home. I remained, in many ways, the "nine-year-old" trying to get the respect and the acceptance from my father. I carried this need into my marriage, my ministry, my profession and my child rearing, and every time I went home, in short, I was stuck. The irony of it all is that my dad did respect and accept me, but on his own terms, as his lack of wellness dictated. He did not know God's design for *paideia*, nor did he understand his very special boy. So, what to do? How could I resolve what I felt in order that I could embrace God's message that would lead to wellness?

Leaving Home

I never spoke about or thought of my dad with disrespect, but when I came to the realization that I was still the boy trying to get his respect and acceptance, I realized that I had never left home. Ephesians 5:31 says that I am to relinquish mother and father and be united with my wife. A boy who emotionally is still at home cannot do this. But how was I to leave home in a way that was healthy?

First, I realized that I had to mourn and grieve that which I will never receive. I can never go back in time to get the things I needed then. I have to grieve those things. They are lost, and even if my father came to me today and put his arm around me and said, "I am so proud of you," it would not take the place of him doing it when I needed it. Grieving these losses, committing them to God and accepting his comfort allows me to leave home.

I have come to see that leaving home is the first step in honoring father and mother. Only then does God rule, and only then do I possess his promise. Leaving home means "wellness upon my life" which enables me to go back home as God's man, able to honor my father and mother—to love them without resentments or reservations.

Why do you have to honor father and mother? Because, according to Scripture, without this there will be no wellness upon your life, and there will be no wellness upon your children's lives. You must trust God, even though you do not want to go there, because your wellness depends on your obedience.

Resolving past issues is a step of faith that allows you to gain the promise of wellness. I believe that one important exercise is to list the things that you feel you missed from your father and mother or the painful things that happened to you as a child. This list will begin to identify the roots of your anger, self-defeating patterns, recurring failures—in other words, the lack of wellness in your adult life. Take the time, however long, to list everything, and then give it all to God. The list is not to send to your parents, but for you to "grieve and leave." If you have not been willing to go there in the past or have denied the reality of having been provoked by the events in your past, now you can begin to be sad, to accept the losses, to receive grace and to be healed. You will take the first step of leaving home and begin to sincerely honor father and mother.

24

Pure Religion
A Father to the Fatherless
Wyndham Shaw

My work as a vice president of HOPE Worldwide has given me the opportunity to travel to many of the most needy places in the world. From India to China and South America to Romania, there are millions of orphans in deep distress because of abandonment and lack of love. One of my goals for life is to champion the cause of adoption and the practice of true religion.

The Need

An estimated thirty million abandoned children live with the wound of being unwanted or at least of not knowing of the love their birth parents have for them. Psalm 68:6 says, "God sets the lonely in families." His heart and his plan is to provide for them emotionally, physically and spiritually. Disciples are the salt of the earth and the light of the world, taught by God to love deeply and from the heart just as he has loved us. When viewed as a whole, the statistic of thirty million orphans sounds overwhelming. But if each of us determines to make a difference one by one—how, where and with whom we can—God's plan for lonely children will be fulfilled.

In China baby girls were once drowned in rivers. Now more than one million are in orphanages and are in need of homes. In India babies are dropped off in cradles that have been set at the doors of orphanages to help prevent mothers from doing away with the babies. More than thirteen million children are in need of homes in that country alone. In Romania more than 150,000 children live in state-run institutions—in a country with a total population of only twenty-three million. Hundreds of thousands of orphans in Cambodia, Russia and Bulgaria—and many other nations in Africa, Latin America and around the world—are distressed and lonely, awaiting God's hand to move on their behalf. Like the lost, these children wait to become the objects of disciples' compassion, benevolence and labors of love.

Jesus championed the cause and innocence of children when he took them in his arms to bless them. He rebuked his disciples for not making time for or giving attention to them. Disciples today must not be guilty of the same neglect and disdain for the children whom Jesus wants to bless. We must let the little children come to us, our homes, our tables, our extra bedrooms and our arms as we become champions of the fatherless, following Jesus in heart and action! Some would say adoption is not for everyone, and I would agree, but it is for many more than have presently accepted God's call in James 1:27:

> Religion that God our Father accepts as pure and faultless is this: to look after orphans and widows in their distress and to keep oneself from being polluted by the world.

True religion is the command of God for all disciples.

There are currently more orphans in distress in the world than at any time in history. We all are responsible before God to take care of orphans and widows in their distress. While traveling throughout the world, I have seen babies lying in their urine and excrement. Children around the world and in our own cities and towns are dying daily of starvation, both physical and emotional. Whether we take them in, contribute money for their care or become big brothers and sisters to those being cared for by others, we cannot obey Scripture or be like Jesus if we do not take care of them in some way.

I am committed to championing orphans by my example, message and ongoing efforts. I applaud the Gempels and many of my fellow geographic HOPE leaders who lead the way in caring for abandoned children through our benevolent programs worldwide.

I also commend the hundreds of disciples who have stepped forward to adopt, such as world sector leaders Doug and Joyce Arthur, Scott and Lynne Green, and Marty and Chris Fuqua; kingdom teachers and their wives, such as Douglas and Vicki Jacoby; evangelists and their wives, such as Mark and Nadine Templer; and hundreds of disciples in churches around the world. I want to challenge many more to step forward this year and in the years to come. Young families need to plan for adopting from the beginning of their marriages. Biological and adoptive blends should become a "norm" among us as we fulfill God's will for orphans.

> **Jesus championed the cause and innocence of children when he took them in his arms to bless them. He rebuked his disciples for not making time for or giving attention to them.**

I also want to commend many single women, such as Joan Lapointe, Katie Scott, Peggy Wells and Donna Bracken, who have pioneered single adoptions and fostering and have found mutual blessings with their children. Single motherhood by choice is a great way to direct the love of our singles to objects of their affection who desperately need what can be so graciously supplied.

Other commendable means of caring for the fatherless that need to be imitated are church adoption funds like the one begun years ago by Randy and Kay McKean in Boston. Randy originated the idea and presented it to the church. Now disciples give more than $100,000 each year to enable disciples to adopt and care for children. More than twenty churches now collect some sort of adoption contribution, but many more need to imitate this example. When leaders lead with such effort, the people willingly offer themselves, and we can all praise the Lord!

The Impact

Tears rolled down my cheeks as I sat in the humble living room of Maria, the elderly lady who lives next door to the orphanage that my son, Jacob, was in. She was telling me how it was through the ten years that she watched the way Jacob and the other children in the orphanage were treated. They grew up in a state institution under the Ceausescu regime and immediately after the fall of Communism in Eastern Europe. She told of how the children would climb the fence as she walked home and reach out their skinny, anemic arms to beg for food. She told of hearing their screams as drunken workers beat them on a whim of anger or frustration. She told of hearing it so loudly one night that she got out of bed and went to the orphanage to ask what they were doing. She was told to go away, but insisted on entering. She stayed until the screaming subsided. She told of befriending Jacob and inviting him over for freshly baked bread and cookies several days a week and of how he would ask if he could bring others to feel and taste her kindness. She told of how Jacob would make sure each new arrival was always grateful and polite, not wanting to risk the loss of the oasis she provided in a physical and emotional desert. Jacob to this day saves money to give to Maria each year when we return to Romania for the HOPE Youth Corps. He calls her several times a month, never forgetting the relief and care she offered in the darkest hours of his existence.

Maria is a small prototype of what adoptive families, HOPE Worldwide programs for abandoned children, and disciples practicing James 1:27 can do. The impact of Jesus' touch and blessing through our arms of love and care is both immediate and eternal. In her book, *Jacob's Journey*, my wife, Jeanie, has effectively recorded many of the ways a family both impacts and is impacted by following Jesus' command to care for orphans. Every family who has adopted can share stories of similar emotion, learning and satisfaction from what happens when we carry out this portion of God's good, perfect and acceptable will.

This chapter expresses the emotional impact that I personally have realized and the memories that this exercise brings up in me. Julia Hannon, Foster Care Director for HOPE Worldwide New England, always says that fostering or adoption has an equally positive impact on both the child and the parents. I believe this is true from both personal and observed experience. It teaches unconditional love, selflessness, patience and appreciation for what being family takes and means to all involved. I have gained fresh gratitude for simple things we enjoy in America, the kingdom and my family just by watching Jacob experience and discover these blessings on a daily basis. Through him I have discovered them again myself. It is like a reconversion of sorts.

Through our HOPE Worldwide group home in Saftica, Romania, I have seen what disciples can create by building a family of love, discipline and spirituality out of seventeen abandoned children brought together by God and his disciples under one roof. Jim and Sarah Bolton, disciples from Springfield, Massachusetts, are doing a heroic job forging a family from a Romanian staff committed to practicing pure religion with these abandoned children. In less than a year the children have gone from being out of control, disrespectful, rebellious and generally dysfunctional to being a true family, expressing affection, self-control, respect and joy with each other.

In November 2000, Jeanie and I had the great joy of assisting in the baptism of Ionela, the oldest girl (sixteen years old) in the home. Randy and Kay McKean, Bob and Pat Gempel, Val and Irene Koha and Bob Tranchell (who oversees our churches in the Balkan States) were able to be there for this crying good time as God adopted for his own one of these abandoned children. Ionela is the first of many such stories of the fatherless being united with their heavenly father. Many more are yet to come as we practice true religion more and more!

The Cost

What does it take to adopt a child, staff an orphanage or run a foster care agency? More than anything, it takes faith, hope and love. It takes faith to believe in something and act on that belief when you cannot see the outcome before you do it. Adopting is scary because you are taking others' biological products and making yourself responsible for what they become. I believe this takes more faith than conceiving our own children whom we know from the womb and who share our blood and genes. Love in adoption is by necessity more of the *agape* or unconditional variety because there is no natural connection drawing us. Adoptive children and foster children do not look, smell or act like you in the way that biological children tend to. Your love is by choice and commitment, and from that comes affection and attraction. It is the same for the child.

Jacob at first did not know what to make of our offering and attempts at love and affection. It was foreign to him and strange. He often would ask, "Why you give me a kiss or a hug?" The great thing is that the longer he has felt it and tried it, the more he likes, relies on and even initiates it. Hope is the ability to persevere because you believe in the eventual positive outcome. Pat Gempel is aptly and affectionately known as "Mama HOPE" by those of us who work with her. She exudes the confidence like few others that we can and will make a difference if we but try and give God room to work.

Hope also springs from the support of those who endure with you through the dark and difficult times of working with orphans who do not always respond quickly or with appreciation to the commitment we make to them. I am no longer naïve about the pain, suffering and plain hard work it takes to care for orphans in their distress. The distress from which they come has not been without effect. They have been wounded and need healing. They have been abandoned and fear it happening again. Parents who take them in must be prepared for the physical, financial, emotional and spiritual challenges they will require. The cross is the ultimate symbol of God's love, not because love is easy, but because it is costly. My challenge would be, for those who hit the painful times of tough love that adoption requires, to not shrink back. Nor should we question why we should take on such a sacrifice. Rather, let us share in the sufferings of Jesus joyfully and with the heart to learn obedience through the things we suffer here as well as in all other aspects of following our Lord!

Equally as important as the heart of sacrifice of those who adopt is the commitment of those who support them, providing not only financial help but whatever else is needed. In Boston we are preparing to launch a postplacement program to supplement our foster care services through HOPE Worldwide New England. The goal of this service will be to provide excellent resources unique to adoptive children that are easily available to our families who have taken in children. The services will include a resource library, art therapy for children, support groups for parents, and seminars to bring in experts in the adoption field to address challenges unique to adoptive families and to provide solutions. Bottom line, anything of value and worth doing will have a significant cost, but our God will and can supply all our needs through his grace and power in Christ (Philippians 4:19).

The Reward

We have gained many rewards by adopting Jacob and by practicing true religion. I think of the simple satisfaction of knowing we practiced James 1:27 in our house, our family and our church. There is the joy of knowing that because we have adopted, others have been encouraged to do so. It is my prayer that Jacob will figuratively become the father of many abandoned children who find families. There is no way we could have seen our family and individual parts of it mature in ways we have without the choice to adopt Jacob.

I believe in my heart of hearts that there will be a special "well done, good and faithful servant!" from the Father and the Son as more and more disciples defend the cause of the fatherless and practice true religion.

This chapter is adapted from the appendix to *Jacob's Journey: One Child's Adoption Teaches Us About Our Place in God's Family* by Jeanie Shaw © 2001 by Discipleship Publications International and is available from DPI at www.dpibooks.org.

Special

Challenges

25

The Challenge of Infertility
Mark Shaw

The second son he named Ephraim and said, "It is because
God has made me fruitful in the land of my suffering."

Genesis 41:52

'I am sorry to have to have to tell you this, but your chances of ever having a child are ten percent at the most." This was the news from my doctor after the results of my fertility tests were in. My wife and I had been trying to get pregnant for almost two years. Karin had already undergone a few tests that revealed no hindrances. She had finally persuaded me to go get tested so that we could really know where our chances stood. I did not expect the problem to lie with me—I suppose I rarely do.

Difficult Times

The last two years had been fairly challenging for us. We had left the ministry staff, were working in new career fields and were doing our best to have impact on the disciples in the congregation. Yet the effort to get pregnant had become very emotionally taxing. Each cycle was accompanied by very high expectations. Karin became deeply discouraged each time it became evident that we were not yet pregnant. And my general response had not been very comforting: "I wouldn't worry about it. It will be alright. God is in control." As you might guess, this neither comforted my wife, nor brought us closer together. I had quite a bit to learn when it comes to being a sensitive husband.

Our romantic life had become more focused on procreating than recreating—not very fulfilling, you can imagine. After receiving the results from my fertility tests, I still remained the happy-go-lucky male: out of touch with my emotions and out of touch with my wife's emotions. "It'll all be okay. We'll just do the next thing on the agenda. Let's find a specialist for fertility."

We started a series of procedures called IVF (In Vitro Fertilization). This involved visiting the hospital to get Karin's blood values tested (approximately every four days) and for her to get a hormone injection (daily). Each of these very strenuous IVF procedures took about two months, plus an extra month to recover. This we did five times over a period of eighteen months. We felt like we were nearly living at the hospital.

It was during this period that I started to crack. I was not even believing my own "it will be alright" statements anymore. This is when I had to go face to face with God. I remember yelling at God during one prayer walk. I felt like even swearing at him! To my surprise, this became a breakthrough for me. I finally was humbled to the point of realizing that not everything was going to just be okay. What if things did not work out? What if we would never have a little girl or boy?

Worse yet, all of this was accompanied by quite a bit of loneliness. Who could relate to what we were going through? To whom do I really feel like explaining the demands of an IVF procedure? Here comes another brother at midweek asking me how I am really doing and how our marriage is really doing. "Thanks for asking, but I don't think you can quite grasp it. I am not convinced that I want to explain a spermiogram to you right now. I am also not sure that I want to tell you that I don't have enough sperm and that those I have are either deformed or sluggish." Please excuse the bluntness, but the feelings of sarcasm were very real.

After deciding to discontinue with IVF we went through another fifteen-month grueling process to be accepted as adoptive parents in Germany. They completely checked us out. They wanted to know everything. These challenges were not easier, just different. But we were more surrendered now than before, more humbled, more in touch. And six months after being accepted, I received a telephone call on the job from Karin, who had just been called by our social worker. She informed us that there was a six-day-old little boy whom we could meet the next day. I remember withdrawing to a small office and just weeping for half an hour. I am weeping right now as I write this. God has given us the most incredible baby in the world. At the time of this writing, he is fourteen months old and is climbing and walking everywhere he can. God truly has displayed his glory in our lives. In a twist of spiritual irony, we have become grateful for our infertility, for we would otherwise never have the boy we have!

Lessons from Joseph

"God is in control" sounds like such good advice—until you are the one whom others are trying to cheer up. Jerry Bridges classic book *Trusting God* helped me immensely throughout this whole experience. I had to keep going back to the scriptures he refers to. These passages became my refuge, the reassurance that God is truly sovereign and always has my best interest as well as his own glory in mind. Regarding the handicapped man in John 9, Jesus said, "This happened so that the work of God might be displayed in his life" (v3). He had his handicap, and I have mine. It may not appear to everyone to be a handicap, but Karin and I had to really wrestle with God to allow him to display his work in our lives.

Infertility is one trial among many. As I look at the great men of the Bible who deeply trusted God throughout their own trials, Joseph stands out. A few lessons from his life seem to apply well.

1. Joseph regarded his circumstances in light of God's providence. He addressed his brothers in Genesis 45:8 with one of the most insightful statements in all the Old Testament: "It was not you who sent me here, but God." Joseph peered through the fog of emotions and beheld the spiritual realm! This conviction guarded Joseph throughout his life. I am confident that he had emotions that cried out, "God, what is your problem? Can't you figure out what you want to do with my life?" Still, he did not allow these feelings to sway him from honoring God in his decision making. How honest have you been with God? King David often got upset with God, only later realizing the hand of God in his circumstances. Although I am ashamed of my accusations toward God, it was exactly these times of honesty in which God helped me to surrender to him.

2. Joseph recognized that God would never leave him (Genesis 39:21-23). He had plenty of reasons to be convinced otherwise: his siblings hated him and plotted his murder, he was banished into slavery in a foreign land, he was falsely convicted of raping a woman, and he was sentenced to a multiyear prison term. Yet, he remained convinced that God was still with him. His automatic response to a question in Genesis 40:8 reveals his close connection to God: "Do not interpretations belong to God? Tell me your dreams." No matter the trials, God has left neither you nor me (James 1:17, Luke 15:31). God has always been there for me; I am actually the one who tends to turn independent and wander off (Matthew 18:12).

3. Joseph relied on God as his only source of hope. He named his first child Manasseh, claiming, "It is because God has made me forget all my trouble and all my father's household" (Genesis 41:51). At this point he never expected to see his family again. I can only imagine the loneliness that Joseph must have often felt. Yet, he allowed this feeling to drive him closer to God, his only refuge.

For us this means seeing how God is working through discipling in our lives. Proverbs 20:5 teaches, "The purposes of a man's heart are deep waters, but a man of understanding draws them out." I had to decide to get and stay open with brothers around me. I could not allow Satan to convince me that my situation is so unique that no one can understand or help me. Let me advise you to find a man of understanding, who can help draw out what is really stirring in your soul.

4. Joseph reasoned that God had a much larger plan for his life. This plan was not completely fulfilled thirteen years later, when Joseph became the right hand to Pharaoh. God waited at least seven more years until he sent Joseph's brothers to him (Genesis 42:6). That was more than twenty years! Genesis 41:51-52 reveals how Joseph was at peace with God and with his own circumstances—long before he would understand the full meaning and depth of God's plan.

How nearsighted and impatient I tend to be! I have to consistently refocus on living daily at peace with God, regardless of whether or not I understand his plan. Having been in the kingdom for almost twenty years now, I am continually reminded by God that I will never outgrow suffering. I am beginning to see how God has allowed Karin and me to endure hardship in order to become a source of encouragement to others facing similar issues (2 Corinthians 1:3-11).

5. *Joseph ran from sin (Genesis 39:15), especially the sin of bitterness.* He not only avoided resentment, but in fact, became a source of encouragement for his enemies. He even comforts his treacherous brothers in the end: "And now, do not be distressed, and do not be angry with yourselves for selling me here, because it was to save lives that God sent me ahead of you" (Genesis 45:5).

Similarly, I needed to guard myself against pulling back from God, my wife and the brothers. Solomon makes it clear in Proverbs, "He who separates himself seeks his own desire, He quarrels against all sound wisdom," (Proverbs 18:1, NASB). It was very reassuring for Karin to know that we were going through this crisis together. It was a shared problem—not just her problem, not just mine. It was especially consoling for me to experience Karin's respect and admiration despite the desperate circumstances.

I had to decide to not leave the responsibilities to my wife, asking her to plan all the medical activities or the adoptive procedures. My closest friends helped regularly remind me to take the lead in these issues. I also needed to focus on being very kind and patient with Karin, especially in light of her regular hormone shots. This was a time that called for wisdom and a gentle tongue. It was important to regularly ask specific questions concerning her thoughts and feelings. Overall, whatever you do, even though it may appear to be founded in sound theology, try to avoid frequent statements such as the one I made: "Well, it'll all be okay."

Fight for Your Faith

All in all, I see how naive I tend to be regarding the spiritual battle. In the midst of pain, it seems impossible to emotionally trust God. Having been in the kingdom for a while, I intellectually understand what is right and therefore try to hang on, letting my experience carry me. Yet, just trying to be a "good and faithful disciple" is never what gets us and our partners through such ordeals. It is rather battling, in the midst of such difficulties, to remain convinced that God is always a good and faithful God!

26

Gaining Perspective Through Depression

Jeff Chappell

And we know that in all things God works for the good of those who love him, who have been called according to his purpose.

Romans 8:28

As you read through Acts and the Epistles, you cannot help but be deeply stirred by the courage and faith of the apostle Paul. He faced imprisonment, beatings, hunger, fear, rejection and so much more on a daily basis. Now consider his declaration: "We know...all things...for the good...." It is not always easy to maintain the perspective that God is working for our good when facing hardships. The past two years have been the hardest of my Christian life. I have been a disciple for more than nineteen years. I have been married and on the ministry staff for fifteen years. About a year ago my wife handed me the book *Rejoice Always*,[1] and in tears said, "I want you to read this." I took the rest of the afternoon and read the whole book. We were both struck by the similarities that I bore to people mentioned in the book who had been diagnosed with depression.

[1] Michael Shapiro, Ph.D. and Mary Shapiro, Ph.D., *Rejoice Always* (Billerica, Mass.: Discipleship Publications International, 2000).

This realization led me to set up an appointment to be professionally evaluated, at which time I was diagnosed with depression and post-traumatic stress syndrome.

This may sound strange, but I was so relieved when I was given this diagnosis. For the past several years I had suspected that something was seriously wrong. No matter what I did, I could not maintain any sustainable joy. I knew I had a terrific wife who loved me, two children who were all I could have wished for and more, and lots of great friends, but still I felt as if I was drowning in an ever-increasing sea of despair. My relief came in knowing that my suspicions had been confirmed; something was wrong.

In the first volume of *A Man in All Seasons*, Tom Jones and Dave Eastman each wrote articles on the subject of depression from their personal experiences. I encourage you to read these articles if you have not done so already.[2] Unlike both Tom and Dave, I have been on medication and have found it to be very beneficial. My goal and hope in writing this article is that it will help those of you who are struggling with depression to gain insight and to get help if you are not currently doing so. I believe with all my heart that God can set us free from the debilitating effects of depression. I am a completely different man than I was one year ago. I still struggle with feeling down, but I am no longer held prisoner to bottomless, dark episodes of depression. I want to share with you what has helped me and how I have come to believe that God does in fact work for our good in all things—even depression.

Nothing to Be Ashamed Of

> But he said to me, "My grace is sufficient for you, for my power is made perfect in weakness." Therefore I will boast all the more gladly about my weaknesses, so that Christ's power may rest on me. (2 Corinthians 12:9)

It can feel like an impossible task, boasting in your weakness when you struggle with depression. Sadly, there is a social stigma that accompanies depression and other forms of mental illness that can lead us to feel ashamed and fearful to tell anyone what we are

---

[2] *A Man in All Seasons—Volume 1*, ed. Thomas Jones, (Billerica Mass.: Discipleship Publications International, 2001) 171-181.

going through. I know a few disciples who exhibit many of the tell-tale symptoms of depression and yet are afraid of being labeled. Some of these symptoms may include insomnia, rapid weight changes, fatigue, persistent anxiety, a sense of worthlessness, preoccupation with thoughts of death or dying, and suicidal thoughts. In my case, I was begging God almost daily to kill me. I was convinced that my wife and kids would be better off without me. Even though I now see these as irrational thoughts (praise God), they did not seem irrational at the time. If you need help, do not be ashamed. Talk to someone. We all need a leg-up from time to time. Get open, and get help!

I am not a medical professional. I offer the following insights concerning medication from personal experience and from information I have gathered in the past year. Medication for depression can be thought of as a kind of catalyst. It provides the extra amount of impetus the brain needs to restore serotonin to normal levels. Serotonin is one of the neurotransmitters in the brain that helps to regulate mood. When we are not producing enough of it, we become depressed. This is treatable and correctable. If you have a chemical imbalance, medication can help. It helped me, and I am not ashamed to have people know this.

> After the service a sister who knows my struggles approached me and told me how moved she had been by the things I shared. Then she said something I will never forget: "Isn't it amazing how so much depth and insight can only come through so much pain?"

Medication for depression does not leave you feeling "high," "up" or "happy." In most cases it take four to eight weeks to determine if a particular medication will work for you. As each person is physiologically different, what works for one person may not work for another. It may take two or three attempts to find the right medication.

The effects of the medication are very subtle. I remember a situation that occurred several weeks after I started my second medication. I reacted with relative calm and with perspective. I remember feeling elated at how I had handled this, realizing the same situation would have been devastating to me only a few weeks earlier.

As Tom mentioned in his chapter in volume one, depression is a complex condition. Medication alone is not the cure. If medication can help you, however, do not feel ashamed. Get proper medical attention. You and your doctor should work together to determine if you should try medication. I believe that, in many cases, it is entirely possible to be cured of depression without medication. I do not believe it is possible to be cured of depression with medication alone. You need to talk and get open about what is going on inside your heart.

Get Out of Isolation

> My friends and companions avoid me because of my wounds;
>   my neighbors stay far away. (Psalm 38:11)

Whether this was true or imagined by David is not all that relevant; it was how he felt. I remember thinking almost verbatim what David expressed above. Depression can leave you feeling like a complete outcast. You do have a choice, however. You do not have to live like a castaway when the riches of the kingdom surround you. Decide that you will trust someone (better yet, a few people) with your thoughts. Trust me, this is a decision, not a feeling.

When I was feeling at my worst, I just wanted someone to understand what I felt without having to explain it to him or her. Jim Lenahen, a brother whom I love dearly, helped me through the roughest times and helped me to see that I had to teach him how to help me. Sometimes people say the wrong things in a genuine attempt to help. I have heard some hurtful things from well-intentioned disciples. Most people cannot completely relate to what it feels like to be clinically depressed, but if we give them a chance, most want to try.

Never stop believing in people's hearts and their sincere desire to help. Do not allow yourself to become isolated from people. If you are trying to help someone who suffers with depression, ask lots of questions and become a great listener. Be willing to try to feel what they feel. This is true empathy.

Stop Trying to Fix Yourself

> Anyone, then, who knows the good he ought to do and doesn't
> do it, sins. (James 4:17)

Christians are fairly proficient at identifying when they have done something wrong or when they failed to do what they should. As a result, we become experts at self-correcting. This is a very dangerous practice when we are not open with others about the negative things we think and do. This is especially true when we have depressive thinking.

One of Satan's most powerful weapons is deceiving us into believing our feelings are true. A great percentage of the thoughts we entertain in a depressed state are contrary to God's word: "I feel God doesn't loves me" or "God has abandoned me." Use your Bible as a weapon and find verses that demolish Satan's lies. Gordon Ferguson taught me an invaluable principle: Do not trust your feelings. Get perspective from others to determine what is true and what is a lie. Decide to live by the admonition of Romans 3:4, "Let God be true, and every man [including yourself] a liar."

James 5:13-16 speaks of the healing power of openness and confession. I believe this verse is meant to imply not only the confession of sin, but also the destructive thoughts and conclusions we often entertain. We must be open about these feelings if we want to get well. How many times have you felt set free after you talked with another disciple about your hurts, feelings, fears, "weird" thoughts or sins? God made us this way. There is a healing that can only take place through openness. Get real, get open and start getting well.

Get Perspective

As I have received help, I have especially had to work through some very hurtful relationships from my past, especially with my father. I had several break-through talks with Mike Leatherwood that taught me how to put my hurts in the past and to rebuild how I think about God and myself. In time I began to feel like a new person. When Christmas came, I had just finished opening presents with my family and started calling my siblings when I learned that my father had died that morning. I will never forget that day. It was very painful to lose my father, but at the same time, I was filled with an incredible sense of God's love. I felt as if he had prepared me for my dad's death by lovingly mending my heart.

Several months later on Father's Day, I gave the message for the Lord's Supper. I talked about my first Father's Day without my dad and how faithful God has been to his promise to give us a hundred times what we could lose (Mark 10:29-30). I read a card I had written to Gordon Ferguson, expressing how grateful I was for the paternal care he had shown me through the months. It is not that I have found a replacement father, but rather, that God has helped to ease the pain of losing my dad by giving me such a caring man who loves me like a son.

After the service a sister who knows my struggles approached me and told me how moved she had been by the things I had shared. Then she said something I will never forget: "Isn't it amazing how so much depth and insight can only come through so much pain?" Pain can bring us closer to God than we ever thought possible if we refuse to allow ourselves to grow bitter because of it. Through our pain we can help others. God has used my experience with depression to help so many people with similar struggles.

God loves us and works for our good. We just need to hang in there long enough to gain that perspective. We were not meant to have lives without pain or trial. We were meant to draw near to God as a result of our pain. We were also meant to be a beacon of light that guides the lost and hurting world into the loving, comforting arms of God. For perhaps the first time in my life, I can say that I am grateful for my struggles because in them, I see God, and through them, his power is made perfect.

27

Dealing with Unemployment
Mark Schnell

"Therefore I tell you, do not worry about your life, what you will eat or drink; or about your body, what you will wear. Is not life more important than food, and the body more important than clothes?...For the pagans run after all these things, and your heavenly Father knows that you need them. But seek first his kingdom and his righteousness, and all these things will be given to you as well. Therefore do not worry about tomorrow, for tomorrow will worry about itself. Each day has enough trouble of its own."

Matthew 6:25, 32-34

Many of us entering the new millennium are children of the "American Dream." Our expectation is to graduate from college and find a well-paying job. Once established in the job market, we expect to get married, have children and ascend the corporate ladder, enjoying all the comforts and security of Western civilization. Along the way, we may plan to be good servants of God and faithful members of his kingdom.

What we can fail to consider is the origin of this dream and whether we have some guarantee of its fulfillment. Unlike the swallows that always arrive in San Juan Capistrano at the migratory calling of their Creator, we sometimes find ourselves arriving at an unseemly destination. This destination may turn out to be a lack of career fulfillment, a tough job market, unemployment and financial debt.

While most of us struggle to comprehend mathematical theory, we have still learned to live our lives relying on statistics and probability. We assume that, by the law of averages, there will always be a job out there for us that will pay what we need and deserve and that our debts will be cleared up in a few short months. Reality is sometimes quite different and quite surprising. Jobs we thought would last for years, sometimes do not. Unemployment we thought would last only a few days, sometimes lasts much longer. Things we thought would surely never happen to us, sometimes do.

> In his heart a man plans his course,
>   but the LORD determines his steps. (Proverbs 16:9)

Few things are more distracting to those who want to keep the kingdom of God first than career changes and unemployment. I know, because my personal employment history includes no fewer than six career changes and five layoffs in a span of only twenty-two years. I had my plans, but God definitely stepped in with some of his own. I learned that in the midst of such challenges, when life seems unstable, when we could easily worry, we need a deep conviction about the God Jesus describes to us in Matthew 6—he is our Creator and knows exactly what is best for us. As our Father, he cares deeply about our needs. He is our King, and his kingdom is the only thing that is unshakable. He tells us that we should not worry about food, clothing or shelter and that we should not chase after these things, (1) because he is very aware of how tempting it is for us to do just the opposite and (2) because we can get all those things and still miss real life. Life may bring some unexpected curves, but Jesus is the one who gives perspective in all the twists and turns.

Career Changes

Career changes are major events in life that often bring with them feelings of anxiety, excitement, challenge or adventure. In some situations, it is exhilarating to know that our talents are needed and desired elsewhere, and the prospect of new relationships and opportunities can far outweigh the risk of the unknown and failure. But these emotions and feelings can be the very foothold that Satan uses to attack and overpower us.

The desire for new challenges, more money, recognition or even a fresh start can tempt us to discard a stable job situation that provides for our family and financially secures our future. What's more, we may know the risk of the change and want it so badly that we avoid seeking advice, fearing that the responses would be "No." Emotionally, we have already made the decision, and the seeking of advice turns out to be nothing more than a perceived need to obtain "permission." In so doing, we lose out on spiritual input that ultimately may guide us away from disaster.

I remember my first career change opportunity...it came less than two years after I graduated from college and started my first career. I had become bored with my job, and an hour-long commute was wearing me out. I received an opportunity over the phone from an employment agency, and I jumped at the chance. What I jumped at was a job relating to aerospace, a twenty-minute commute and a negligible increase in pay. Looking back now, I can see how emotional a decision it really was, because I sought no advice, and I walked away from the best-paying career I would probably ever have.

Now as a disciple, I am much less vulnerable to the temptations that pulled at me that first time because my career is now a very small piece of a large picture. In Christ I have a hope and a future, and my purpose is to deny myself, take up my cross daily and follow Jesus. As I lead my own family to Christ and give myself to others, I find that I need stability in my career, not adventure and challenge. Without Jesus, I would have no purpose, and my career would become perhaps the center of my life.

> Do nothing out of selfish ambition or vain conceit, but in humility consider others better than yourselves. (Philippians 2:3)

Pursuing a career change may be necessitated by a layoff, a need to relocate for family reasons, or perhaps a call by God into or out of the ministry. But when the desire to change careers is motivated by personal desires, we need to humbly accept the facts that (a) God is much more capable of guiding our steps, and (b) there are others who are able to more objectively test our motives and the ramifications of the change. If the desired change will take more of our time away from our family and give us less time to work in the kingdom, it is likely a trap of Satan. If the perceived need for more money is based on the love of things, or if the desire for personal recognition comes from bad relationships at home or in the church, then we are failing to trust God and put the kingdom first.

My career has changed from automotive production engineering to aerospace quality assurance, to ministry training, to microelectronics, to technical writing/training, to supplier quality assurance, and currently to quality assurance management. Many hard lessons were learned along the way. My decision to leave engineering and pursue the ministry was fueled by my heart to serve God, but my failure to seek advice resulted in severe financial challenges that still affect my daily life. But I thank God that he gave me a strong and faithful woman as my wife, partner and friend, whose advice and counsel is focused on God.

Layoffs

In times of financial challenge, companies often find the laying off of employees as an effective (albeit unpleasant) means of reducing costs and thereby securing the future of the company. Our jobs generate a source of steady income for our families, a comfortable environment for sharing our faith and even a means of building personal self-esteem. When we are summoned to the human resources department to receive that pink slip, the experience can feel like a literal punch in the stomach. After a brief period of shock and then anger, we become overwhelmed with all manner of thoughts and feelings. What if my attendance was better? What if I had gotten my reports in on time? Why didn't I take those night courses? Will my family lose confidence in me? What will we do for money? Why have you forsaken me, God?

But God has not forsaken us. As he said to the Jews in Jeremiah's day, he says to us:

> "For I know the plans I have for you," declares the LORD, "plans to prosper you and not to harm you, plans to give you hope and a

future. Then you will call upon me and come and pray to me, and
I will listen to you. You will seek me and find me when you seek
me with all your heart." (Jeremiah 29:11-13)

As a liar and the father of lies (John 8:44), Satan wants nothing
more than for us to believe that God is harsh and unloving and out
to punish us for each and every sin we commit. Nothing could be
further from the truth. God is the best of all fathers, and he is constantly guiding our steps on paths and through situations that will
bless and enrich us. A layoff just might be the very situation that will
enable you to crash through the barrier of mediocrity and move forward in courage and faith and forever change your life.

So, how do I deal with a layoff? Am I to come home humming
a merry tune with the contents of my office in a cardboard box?
That's not likely, especially when I really feel like running away or
indulging myself in the sins that are swirling through my mind.
Like any test from God, my heart should be drawn toward God for
help, as a drowning man gropes for a life preserver. As one who has
endured no less than five layoffs since I became a disciple of Jesus,
allow me to offer a few practicals.

- **DO**...Pray—pray—pray. Before dropping the bombshell on
  your family, find a quiet place to pray. When you are feeling
  shaken, do whatever it takes to get connected to the One who
  is unshakable.
- **DO**...try to reach an elder, evangelist or other strong brother in
  Christ for comfort and advice, especially if they have been
  through layoffs themselves. Try to do this before you go home
  to talk to your family about it.
- **DON'T**...walk in the door and say, "Guess what, honey? I got
  laid off!" Remember that you are the spiritual leader of your
  family and that God is about to bless your life. As you share the
  news, you need to both feel their pain and give them an
  example of faithfulness to follow.
- **DO**...humbly formulate a plan. A normal after-shock of a
  layoff is a numbing apathy. We can feel ill-equipped to deal
  with it all and feel that we need time to heal. It is, rather, the
  time for us to put on the armor of God (Ephesians 6:11-18) and
  fight off Satan's attack. Go to the unemployment office the next
  morning. Prepare and/or update your resume. Make a list of

your best contacts and start networking. (If you do not know how to do these things, have a brother or sister show you.) Search the Web for employment opportunities. And while you wait for God's answer to your prayers, use your temporary newfound free time to serve others.

• **DON'T**...make any compromises with righteousness. Be honest when reporting any income from part-time jobs to the IRS. Don't ask your family to go without while you spend more time on the golf course. Perhaps, for now, you won't be able to keep your financial pledge to the kingdom, but don't be tempted to discontinue giving altogether. Remember that God blesses you in more ways than your weekly paycheck. How can God bless you when you act in faithlessness? Seek plenty of advice, look for ways to sacrifice (cancel cable TV, subscriptions and other discretionary spending), and then give with a heart like the widow who was commended by Jesus (Luke 21:1-4).

God Is Good

> Trust in the LORD with all your heart
> and lean not on your own understanding;
> in all your ways acknowledge him,
> and he will make your paths straight. (Proverbs 3:5-6)

Remember those five layoffs I referred to earlier? Believe me, Satan has tempted me to conclude that the layoffs after my decision to follow Jesus are proof that God does not have my best interests in mind. However, with an amazing woman at my side and a deep conviction that God loves me, I have grown to see how incredibly God has acted on my behalf. Remember how I went into deep debt after following my heart to pursue the ministry years before? Each layoff resulted in a significant raise, and the longest time between jobs was only ten weeks. And each new job added a dimension to my resume that would ultimately open the door for the next job! And while Satan was snickering at my troubles, God was, in reality, helping me to pay off the debt and building my faith in the process.

When I consider all the decisions that I have made in my forty-three-plus years of life, by far the hardest was made after my fourth layoff. I had begun to see how God was blessing us through the lay-offs and career changes, and this time, I felt equipped to handle this one on my own. For the first time, I was faced with not one, but two job offers to choose from, both at identical salary levels.

One job offer came from a company in Rhode Island that was growing through company acquisitions, and the president wanted me to join their team as their new quality manager. The other job offer came from a company only forty minutes away from our home, but they wanted me to be a supplier engineer, a career step back for me. My personal ministry was stale and unfruitful, and having spent five years previously in Rhode Island, I believed that the family and friends there would give us a hero's welcome. I could taste the prestige of the new position in the aggressive, growing company. Still, my heart struggled, and I felt a strange guilt about leaving my local church and family group. Fortunately, I decided not to lean on my own understanding.

I called Kevin McDaniel, my lead evangelist and a man I thoroughly respect and trust, and sought his advice. I half-expected him to say, "No, you shouldn't leave," but rather, he asked me why I believed that God had led me to Methuen, Massachusetts, in the first place. I thought for a moment, and I recalled my conviction, that he brought me to Methuen so that my kids could grow in the strong teen ministry in that region of the Boston church. Kevin stressed that the decision was mine and that he would support my choice, but he advised me to make sure I was seeking the kingdom first. I hung up the phone, and I cried some of the bitterest tears I'd ever cried. The decision was the hardest I would ever make—but it was also the simplest. What *I* wanted was far less important than what my family needed. So, I took that lesser job…and my son Steve was baptized soon afterward. And layoff number five? It enabled me to take my current job as (oddly enough) a quality manager for a growing company…only twelve minutes from our home—God is good!

Career changes? Layoffs? While such things may weigh on us, in Christ, these are merely trivial pursuits compared with trusting God and following the straight paths he is mapping out for us. To God be the glory!

28

Bringing a Brother Back
Doug Cameron

The archangel Michael was sitting on a bench in the early Midwest sun, his eyes closed to the rising light. It would be obvious to anyone looking at him that he was conflicted. "Hmmm...it's going well." As he spoke to the dog next to him, his face was contorted in the manner of someone in deep contemplation. "It's a difficult case, though," he said as he shook his head, "*to give a man back his heart.*" And we, the observers, finally begin to understand why he was here on this, his final visit to our world, from his world in heaven.

"To give a man back his heart...." That is what bringing a brother back to God is all about, isn't it? This scene is from one of my favorite movies, *Michael*. While the premise and content are not very Biblical, I fell in love with the idea that God would do something so grand as to send his very best warrior, his best angel, on his last visit to earth for the sole purpose of giving a man his heart back. It is very close to the message of the gospel. As the writer of Hebrews points out, the one who came was far superior to angels. He was the Son.

Why is it so difficult to move a man's heart? Our female counterparts can cry over a long-distance-telephone advertisement on television. Men, on the other hand, have a shell of hardness around their hearts. Every one of us is built with a resistance to vulnerability and change—I am convinced of that. To touch a man's heart, we must look at who we are, fundamentally.

Who Are These Creatures?

I believe two words describe us men very well: *prideful* and *insecure*. Every man alive is imbued with these characteristics. Try not to look at these words initially with a negative view. Instead, understand that these are both variants of a purpose within us, a God-given purpose to lead and protect. Our society, as advanced as we like to think we are, still reinforces these instincts within us. Even as Christians, we look more favorably upon the outwardly confident man than we do the vulnerable man. Some men know that their pride and their insecurities (which are forms of pride) are the springboards for sin. They are aware of these, the thorns in the flesh, and use them to remind themselves of the need to have a soft heart, to remain humble and to stay close to their Father in heaven.

> **"To give a man back his heart...."**
> **That is what bringing a brother back to God is all about.**

Most of us, however, are not like this! We ritually and habitually engage in all kinds of behaviors that are uniquely male, in order to preserve the protection this shell of hardness gives us.

Is it easy for you to be open and vulnerable with your leader after he makes a joke at your expense in a group setting? Nope! Can you not just hear the leader's response to your defensiveness: "Oh…it's a guy thing. Lighten up! We ought to be able to poke fun at one another without getting upset. In fact, it's a bonding experience, done in love. You *know* I love you, don't you?" And the occasion sticks in your craw, because deep inside, the hurtful comment only reinforces the idea that you are worthless or something to be laughed at. Your insecurity rises, and then, wonder of wonders, the hard shell grows thicker. Yes, it's a guy thing all right.

Or, perhaps you work hard at your career or job. In fact, your wife and discipling partner tell you that you work *too* hard. You work hard enough to know that you can take immense pride in what you do. You make a good living—after all, isn't that what a good Christian husband and father does, provide for his family?

And when you hear the NASDAQ drop lower, your first reaction is anger and self doubt.

Maybe you knew shame long ago when your family grew up poor, or when your father drank too much and beat you. Though you felt freed from the *guilt* of your own sin when you were baptized in Christ, the *shame* from growing up has not left you. And when the stock market sinks a bit or a toilet overflows in the upstairs bathroom or the car breaks down, the shame hits you once again, and your family sees, once again, your frustration and anger. So, you go back to work, that place you can take pride in. Understanding who we are, as men, is vital to leading men to Christ and back to Christ…again and again.

Why Do Men Leave?

Why do men leave the church and God? The simple answer is—we have to *find out* why! Everybody has a reason. All too often, the response I will get when I ask why someone has left is: "They just weren't committed enough" or "They decided they loved the world more than they loved God." Each of these statements may be very true, but they are not enough. It is like saying, "Because their hair is brown." It's an obvious truth, but it tells me nothing about what went on inside the man's head; it tells me nothing about why that man thinks that leaving the family of God is a choice he must make. The Bible makes it clear: There *is* no life outside of Christ! Therefore, why would he choose to forsake that? Do you assume you know why someone left the church? Have you asked him what he felt, what he went through, why he made that choice? We must ask the questions—and *listen* to the answers.

Listening

Listening is a lost art; I am convinced of that. Listening means that I am not talking. (Sounds simple, doesn't it? You'd be surprised….) But listening is more. Listening means that I am engaged. Listening means that I do not interrupt because I have a point of view that is shouting within me. Listening means that I am actively trying to understand what the other person is saying. I may not agree with his line of thinking, but I try to understand what he is saying. Listening means that I communicate my understanding by nodding my head and by asking clarifying questions in a nonthreatening way. Listening means that I validate the person's feelings, even if I do not agree with his view on events.

Bottom line, listening is *hard work* (James 1:19). I have failed many times at listening to someone, especially when I am personally involved in the events they are describing. But, like any skill, it can be practiced. Practice listening. Know when to talk, as there are those times when you need others to listen to you. But when it is your turn to listen—be quiet and listen!

How skillful of a listener are you? There is really only one way to find out. Ask ten or twelve of your closest friends—both male and female (and don't forget your wife!).

Duct Tape Discipleship

Another way our pride shows up is in how we always want to provide *solutions*. We love 'em, which is why we love Home Depot. If we have a problem, there's nothing that a quick trip to Home Depot will not fix. One of our favorite hardware store products is duct tape—a wonderful invention, because it fixes almost everything! (I knew a brother who was going to write a book titled *1001 Uses for Duct Tape!*) Similarly, we like to solve others' problems for them.

Those of us who are married have learned that our wives, of course, do not want their problems to be fixed. They especially do not want a piece of duct tape put on their problems—it does not help them at all. Amazingly, they do not even want us men to come up with solutions for them. You may be wondering why women bring up issues at all? It's because they like to process their feelings aloud; it is their God-given way to resolve issues—without duct tape.

Believe it or not, I think that our experience with our wives and the women in our lives should help us to better relate to each other as men. Most men I know who are trying to restore the faith they once had, do not want quick fixes either. They do not want to hear the quick spiritual diagnosis and get the spiritual prescription for their particular malady. When they are listened to and feel understood, they have a much better chance of listening to God themselves. In fact, they probably already have a pretty good idea of the steps they need to take to get back to God, but what they really need is someone to walk that path with them, through the Scriptures. Again, without duct tape.

When we try to quickly give solutions, we are a lot like the man in Proverbs 27:14 who loudly blesses his neighbor early in the morning. We may mean well, but what we do is not really helpful. Do you resist the desire to quickly diagnose and fix someone's feelings? Asking those around you is really the only way to know how you are doing with this.

The Word of God

One of the hardest things for me to do is to consistently go back to the word of God when I counsel others. It may be easier for some, but it is hard for me. In my experience, it is hard for most men. We love to hear our own voices (remember our pride?), and we fail to consistently use Scripture to preach, to be prepared, to correct, to rebuke and to encourage. We miss the point of restoring someone gently (Galatians 6:1) by being spiritual (as in Holy Spirit, as in Author of the Scriptures).

One of the highlights of my week is getting together with Jack Frederick and Tom Jones as fellow elders in the Northwest region of the Boston church. Tom has faithfully disciplined Jack and me to listen to God first, by always reading a passage together at the beginning of our time. Sometimes it is hard because when we get together, there is so much to talk about. And yet, nothing is more important or more meaningful than those few minutes spent reading Scripture together.

This is why Bible discussion groups are so effective. Where else do we get a chance to be in a relaxed atmosphere, read Scripture, hear others be open about their lives, talk about how this passage relates to us, and feel like we have been vulnerable to the point of letting God into our hearts? The word of God is what brings about faith, men. No amount of talking, spiritual diagnosing or amateur psychology will bring about the faith that God produces through his word (Romans 10:17).

How often do you open the Bible outside of quiet times? Do you ever read a passage with a brother, just for encouragement's sake? Do you share passages that delight you with those around you? To bring a man back to God, you must get him back to the word of God.

Believe in Me

Jesus asked his disciples to believe in him (John 14:11). Of course, he had been believing in *them* for a long time. What could possess Jesus to take this bunch of sorry, selfish, uneducated, rag-tag, attitudinal, fickle derelicts and give them the keys to the kingdom of God? It sure does not sound like a great way to start a ministry to me! How could he endure the mistakes and worldliness they got into? How would a leader grow a church without sharp, spiritual people who are going to lead?

The answer, I believe, is that it is the Holy Spirit, working through the word of God, working through men's hearts, who causes a ministry to become active and vibrant and growing. In the same way, it is the Holy Spirit who sees far beyond what we can see with our earthly eyes, who searches our hearts for signs of love for God. It is the Spirit at work through God's grace that teaches us to say "No!" to ungodliness (Titus 2:12), and the Spirit that causes our hearts to turn from self to the cross (1 Corinthians 12:3). Jesus did not see those twelve with human eyes; he saw them through the lenses of the Holy Spirit. Jesus believed in them. He believed that they would glorify God with their lives—even Judas!—and that he and the Father and the Holy Spirit would give them exactly what they needed to start a *revolution of faith*. Though prideful Peter walked away in fear from his faith, Jesus saw him and believed in him as the man to lead his followers after he had made his way to heaven.

Do you think it important to believe in others? What are the ways that others feel believed in by you? Do you have the heart that the writer of Hebrews expressed to his readers: "Even though we speak like this, dear friends, we are confident of better things in your case—things that accompany salvation" (Hebrews 6:9). The man you are bringing back to God needs to hear that kind of message from you.

The Mess

Understanding who we are as men, asking candid questions, listening, not being prone to quick fixes, depending on the word of God, and believing in people are all important in helping a man wade through the mess of restoring his relationship to God. Yes, the *mess*—it gets ugly sometimes! In my opinion, the most frequently encountered issue in helping a heart grow close to God again is to resolve the issues of personal relationships within the body of Christ. We all expect to have poor relationships in the world, and we expect great relationships within the kingdom. Alas, all we are promised from God is the opportunity to make relationships better, the chance for hard work to bring about strength in the bonds that tie us together. Unfortunately, we often forget about the hard work part! Resolving issues with other disciples, especially leaders, is so important. It was vital to almost every man I have seen be restored to faith. Again, our pride and insecurities will often stop us from engaging the hard times of "working it out," so it is very important to have someone alongside us, walking with us step by step—someone we trust and has demonstrated the qualities we have discussed above.

Think about and talk about the experiences the man wanting to be restored had as a Christian, both good and bad. What do you think his issues will be? How will you help him to think about them? Scripture describes the reaction of heaven to a restored brother in the most dramatic of terms. It is the time for rejoicing in heaven (Luke 15:7, 10). It is a time for extravagant celebration (Luke 15:22-23). Bringing a brother back to God will cost you, but who can even estimate the worth?

Passages to Dwell On

- 1 Corinthians 1—Who are we as Christians?
- Galatians 5 and 6—How does the Holy Spirit work within me?
- 2 Timothy 4:1-8—How should we view God's word in helping others?
- 1 John 4—What is perfect love, and what does fear have to do with me?
- Philippians 2:1-11—What is true humility?
- Ephesians 4:1-16—What are the building blocks of unity?
- 1 Peter 5:1-11—How does Satan hurt us?
- Proverbs 1-9—How do I listen to God and to others?

29

Help for Those Being Restored
Steve Major

*T*he promises of Christianity are not true. The Bible says that I can have *life to the full, complete joy, intensely deep relationships and more.* In ten years of trying as a disciple, I had only caught faint glimpses of some of these promises. I knew that there was a God and that he was at work in all our lives. I had grown to believe that God was going to use the church to proclaim his message and do his bidding. I knew I was involved in God's perfect plan, but the plan did not pan out to be perfect for me. To me, the promises of Christianity were not true.

God or Me?

I wondered where all the victories were that I had been told so much about. I wondered why I was not experiencing all the things that we should experience as Christians. I spent years of my life feeling the same way that I imagine the woman at the well felt in John 4. When she realized that Jesus was a prophet, she seemed to ask about something she had been longing to see for a long time— she wanted to know about true worship. Her previous experiences must have been disappointing. Whether in Jerusalem or in Samaria, the promises of God did not seem to be true for her. She was downcast and disappointed, and it did not seem like much was going to change anytime soon; yet deep inside, she longed to see the kingdom of God and to see the fulfillment of the promises that she had heard about.

It seems to me that there are a great number of Christians who feel this way. Some have felt this way for so long that they have given up the fight and perhaps have stopped believing that Christianity is true at all. I contend that most of the people who fall away do so because of disappointments. I left God's church in 1995, frustrated, confused and feeling alone. I thought that I had a deep love for God and that the reason I was falling away was because I was tired of being a hypocrite. Now, as I look back from a different perspective, I know that I did love God, but I did not love him more than I loved myself. I didn't love him enough to relinquish my fears. I didn't love him enough to close my back doors, nor to accept the things I couldn't understand (that I should have accepted simply because he said they were so). I didn't love him enough to give up my lust or my irresponsibility. When I look back on my life in the kingdom prior to being restored, I think Jesus was warning me in Luke 14 when he demanded that I must hate "even [my] own life." I was not experiencing Christianity because I was not working out my end of the bargain. Consequently, my Christianity was a drain, and I felt enslaved.

Running in the Wrong Direction

If I had experienced life to the full in the kingdom (John 10:10), there would have been no reason for me to leave. The bottom line of why I fell away in 1995 was because God had plans for my life, and I had different plans. Even now, many in the kingdom are afraid that God's plans for their lives are different than their own plans. For example, forgiving people when they have wronged you is a difficult thing to do; nevertheless, this is a part of God's perfect plan for you (Matthew 18:21-35). I have had to learn that many of us need to be told how hurtful or destructive our actions are, and my brothers and sisters may need to be told by people like me. I see now that God brings people together—sinful people—so that we can speak his words to each other (Ephesians 4:15) and help each other get the healing that we so desperately need (Proverbs 12:18).

I have also learned that impurity, pride, insecurity and even loneliness are all things that I tend to run to when life gets tough and scary. It seems like such a dichotomy that the things I run to when I need the most help are the very things that destroy what I desire most in life: deep, abiding, aware relationships. These sins have become some of my "best friends," because they are always there in my life, just waiting for me to give them a call.

Trust 101

Before I left the church, I often said that I was doing well as a Christian. I put up fronts, all the while sharing my faith. I kept sins hidden. In reality I am terrified of opening my heart up to others, thus giving them the power to hurt me. Sometimes, I imagine that they will look down on me, chide me, abandon me or in other ways hurt me.

As I opened up to coming back, I learned from my studies with Jim Valente (and a host of others) that God counters my fears with a call to trust. My fears were based on the fact that if I were to expose my weaknesses, men would be able to harm me. This type of thinking is a diabolical plan of Satan, because it completely removes God from the picture. Even if men harm me, God has promised, "Never will I leave you, never will I forsake you." He is a refuge from the storms of life, and David says:

> I lie down and sleep;
> I wake again, because the LORD sustains me.
> I will not fear the tens of thousands
> drawn up against me on every side. (Psalm 3:5-6)

Even the fact that I wake up in the morning is testimony to God's faithfulness. Though there are ten thousand that may oppose me, God is able to rescue me. I can take comfort in this because the Lord shows every day that he is about the work of sustaining me. I've been praying to believe that, and I still pray to believe that. Nahum 1:7 says "The LORD is good, a refuge in times of trouble. He cares for those who trust in him" and Psalm 52:8 says:

> But I am like an olive tree
> flourishing in the house of God;
> I trust in God's unfailing love
> for ever and ever.

As I have come back to God and his kingdom and started to learn to trust, I see that the only way to flourish in life is to trust in God's love for me. Even still, I wrestle with trusting God with my whole heart, but I am learning to trust him with even my deepest desires. Things that I hope for my life may be taken away, or never acquired, but I must know that God wants and will do what is best for me in every situation. As I write this, I am wrestling in my heart, because it is almost like a literal letting go of things that I hold dear. I have hopes for relationships, for status, for financial and vocational position. But trust means letting go.

When I started really trusting, my life began to feel like "life to the full" (John 10:10). As I venture out and attempt greater openness, I find that it is met with understanding more often than not. Typically, people that I confess the most difficult things to turn right around and relate completely to what I tell them with grace and understanding.

Unstuffing

This is a far cry from where I was at spiritually six years ago when I fell away. Life may or may not have changed appreciably, but my approach to life has totally changed. I have learned to pray when times get tough, although it might take a while before I see my need to pray. Before I go to prayer, I typically will stew for a bit, hide in my computer and work for awhile (my girlfriend says that I am going into my cave), and then I realize that my mind and heart have to change. The psalmist captures my feelings on paper:

> When I tried to understand all this,
>   it was oppressive to me
> till I entered the sanctuary of God;...
> When my heart was grieved
>   and my spirit embittered,
> I was senseless and ignorant;
>   I was a brute beast before you. (Psalm 73:16-17, 21-22)

This is precisely what happens to me now. I become a brute beast that hides in a cave. In the past there was no way out of the cave. Now I have relationships with people who can understand the things I go through. There are a host of men that I can call that can relate, empathize, challenge, comfort or rebuke if necessary. Unfortunately, openness seems to be coming in stages. I would like to say that I am open like a book, but I'm not. I'm still timid and afraid of what people will think. Consequently, I pray every day not to give in to my fears.

Patience

I have learned that I have to be okay with growth in stages. Paul encouraged his young disciple, Timothy, to "be diligent...so that everyone may see your progress" (1 Timothy 4:15). In the past, I expected my life to be like the apostle Paul's life, complete with blinding lights and voices from heaven (Acts 9:1-4). I think that these expectations are some of the reasons that I was not open with my life; I was afraid to shatter the image others had of me (that was present only in my mind, by the way!). I'm learning that the path to growth is a mixture of relationship with God, the Scriptures, relationships with others and time.

We cannot be afraid of the time element in our growth. A decision I had to make when being restored was to take as much time as was necessary. As I studied and prayed with the posse of brothers that God marshaled to help me conquer my fears, there was never a shortage of people to ask things like, "So when are you going to get right with God?" But I had to be sure that I was acting on my convictions, not theirs. That only came with time.

Helping Others

Lastly, I had to learn that even falling away could be used to help others. Jesus told the original Twelve, "This very night you will all fall away on account of me" (Matthew 26:31). Then later Jesus said:

> "Simon, Simon, Satan has asked to have all of you, to sift you like wheat. But I have pleaded in prayer for you, Simon, that your faith should not fail. So when you have repented and turned to me again, strengthen and build up your brothers." (Luke 22:31-32 NLB)

Since falling away and returning, I have been able to speak to others who have thought about the same and are terrified to articulate their thoughts. I understand their fears. Everyone has a place in the family of God, but only if they decide that it is to be so. All of us are weak in different areas of our lives. All of us need strengthening. I've learned that I am needed here because God has a plan. People can absolutely go from being deserters to being powerful strengtheners of others. Just look at these before and after snapshots of John Mark and get inspired!

> Barnabas wanted to take John, also called Mark, with them, but Paul did not think it wise to take him, because he had deserted them in Pamphylia and had not continued with them in the work. (Acts 15:37-38)

> Only Luke is with me. Get Mark and bring him with you, because he is helpful to me in my ministry. (2 Timothy 4:11)

30

Facing Terminal Illness
Fighting the Good Fight
Ben Weast with Jeff Marco

*T his chapter was written by Ben Weast about his friend Jeff Marco
shortly before Jeff's death which came on April 29, 2001. Ben's conversation with Jeff and his wife, Lila, give us many powerful perspectives.*

> For I am already being poured out like a drink offering, and the
> time has come for my departure. I have fought the good fight, I
> have finished the race, I have kept the faith. Now there is in store
> for me the crown of righteousness, which the Lord, the righteous
> Judge will award to me on that day—and not only to me, but to
> all who have longed for his appearing. (2 Timothy 4:6-8)

I know a man whose life has been lived as a "drink offering," a
man who has a fought an incredible fight, who has kept his faith in
the face of prolonged suffering. I know a man whose race toward
the throne of God our Father is nearing its completion; a man who,
though full of love for his family, the kingdom and the lost, is eager
to receive his crown from the Eternal God. Jeff Marco *is* that man!

A Suffering Servant

I have known Jeff for nearly twenty-five years. In the mid-
1970s, both of us developed our fledgling, spiritual wings in the
campus ministry at N.C. State University. Jeff, a quiet, intense man
with a dry wit and a pioneer's faith, has rarely been a public leader.

He is the behind-the-scenes servant on whom the public leaders rely to move the kingdom forward. He is the epitome of the Biblical principle of going anywhere, doing anything and giving up everything for Jesus.

Jeff moved his family several times over the years so that they could be where the kingdom needed them the most or in order to get spiritual help for himself and his family. Jeff and his wife, Lila, have been married for more than twenty-one years and have three sons: Aaron, a freshman at Duke University, Brian, a high school sophomore and Christopher, a fourth grader. Blessed with a gift for administration, Jeff's wisdom has helped many families right their sinking financial ships. He was instrumental in mapping out the development plans for the Triangle church property and facilities. All these things he has done under the umbrella of making disciples. There are many people who would not be in the Triangle church without Jeff's faith and perseverance.

Jeff and his family have personified faith and perseverance during the last five years. After experiencing several health problems in 1994 and 1995, Jeff was diagnosed with Peritoneal Mesothelioma on January 15, 1996. Since this is a rare form of cancer with no standard treatment, Jeff's physicians gave him only months to live. Many would have crumbled and lost hope, but during the last four and a half years, Jeff has built a legacy of faith in God. During this time he has seen the completion of the church's main auditorium, pavilion and ball field complex. Most importantly, he has seen his two eldest sons become disciples of Jesus, Aaron in February 1997 and Brian in February 2000.

When it appeared that the cancer would claim Jeff quickly, he wrote letters of faith, love and encouragement to each of his sons. Thinking he would already be gone, these letters were to be read at each of his son's baptisms. So far, Jeff has lived to see two of them read their letters. Recently, I talked with Jeff and Lila about their lives, and they shared with me some wisdom acquired during the past five years.

Urgency

Jeff believes that a disciple needs to be urgent. He described for me a mental game he plays called, "Sixty seconds to die—what do you pray for?" He said the game revealed his heart. "I did not pray first for my wife and my family, but rather myself," Jeff said. He now sees life as an exercise in urgency! He says, "I don't have tomorrow; I've got to express myself; I've got to repent today—get my house in order, sharing my faith as I go."

Jeff and Chris had a conversation regarding the N.C. state fair. The Marcos usually go as a family to the fair each year, and Jeff told Chris that he probably would not be physically able to go to the fair with them this year. Chris responded, "Dad, that doesn't matter; I'm so glad I have you around, just to come and talk to you." Many conversations with Chris have been triggered by statements Chris has made like, "My daddy teaches me about the Bible, and I won't have that when he dies"; "Daddy if you die, who is going to baptize me?"; and "When Daddy dies, and I have a big problem, how can I get to where he is so I can talk to him?"

Jeff appreciates every opportunity he gets with his sons. "Chris has been so respectful and warm lately. On a recent Monday morning, he got up around 3:00 A.M. to use the bathroom. Coming back, he noticed that I was sitting up, so he came and cuddled with me for about ten minutes. It was a very special moment."

Jeff has a very sober message, particularly for parents: "I'm only losing a little bit of time on you. You'll be where I am before you know it. Prepare for it. Get your own house in order, *now!*"

Desperation

Living through Jeff's suffering has taught Lila and the family to be desperate for God and to see the desperation in the lives of others. She said, "From the onset of Jeff's cancer people, have been conscious of how desperate our family has been for God to work, but in fact all people are just as desperate everyday for God to work in their lives, to give them breath. We just don't acknowledge it."

While sharing his faith early in his illness, Jeff asked some people if they would trade places with him and of course, they declined the offer. Several of them have already died before him. Jeff's illness has taught the family to be grateful for each day, for each other and for all that God has given them. To young people who want to do drugs or attempt suicide, Jeff has wanted to exclaim, "Take my body and give me yours! Do you appreciate what you have? Nothing ails you that you can't get over."

Suffering Produces Character

As we continued to talk, Jeff said, "I've learned to love my cancer, because the suffering and perseverance have changed my character." I thought to myself, "Wow!" and then 1 Peter 1: 6-9 came to mind. I realized that I was sitting with a man every bit as faithful as Job! Jeff spoke of his and his family's response to his disease and impending death. "It has forced me to face fears. It has redefined me. Who am I going to be in the process of dying? It has matured me when I seek honor and dignity rather than lapse into whiny, wimpish complaining: 'Okay, I hurt everyday—big, hairy deal!'"

Jeff spoke affectionately of the Holy Spirit saying, "I have come to appreciate the Holy Spirit and his power, and I have learned to let him work rather than quench him as I have done in the past."

Grieving Vs. Self-Pity

Lila added to Jeff's thoughts by sharing what she was learning about grieving. She said that self-pity is a "line that we don't have to cross, but it's easy to cross." She has learned to see when she is falling into this trap by catching thoughts like, "This shouldn't be happening to me!"

Early in his illness, while driving home from the hospital and feeling very sleepy she thought, "What if I have an accident and I die too! God, that would not be fair! We've had our share of suffering." She realized that though this was a natural response, it was not spiritual! She asked herself, "Do I really believe that God is in control? Do I trust that he will see me through this?" She said that she realized something very powerful at this point, "Anytime you go to feeling sorry for yourself, you've gotten prideful, feeling, 'I'm too good for this!'" She continued by saying, "You can't put limits on God. Let him work!"

Lila learned recently that she had a lesion in her breast that needed to be removed, but she was able to hold on to her conviction and not worry about the outcome.

She has also learned what true grieving is. She describes it this way, "This is sad and it hurts, but this is part of God's creation and he will comfort us in it. It hurts him too."

Answered Prayers

Jeff and Lila shared about many prayers that God had answered, particularly over the last five years. The prayers revolved around his illness and the success of experimental treatments, the growth of their marriage, the conversion of their sons, and the growth of the Triangle church and God's movement as a whole. They believe in prayer and its power to bring people closer to God. According to Jeff, their perspective is summed up in the following example. Recently, six-year-old Mattie (Madison) Millis asked her father if Jeff was going to die. When her father responded "Yes," she exclaimed, "I've been praying for Jeff to live; doesn't God listen to my prayers?" When Jeff heard about this, his response was, "God has answered 'Yes,' everyday for four and a half years. One day he will say, 'No.' God increases our faith with a thousand days of 'Yes' and one day of 'No.'"

The Effect on the Family

I can only imagine the intensity with which the Marco family has struggled to remain close, let alone grow closer to God and to each other during Jeff's illness. Jeff and Lila are the first to tell you that there have been times of tremendous emotional, physical and spiritual stress within their home, and the picture has sometimes not been pretty. There have been moments when it seemed like their family was going to explode beyond repair. "But God," as Jeff would say, has been working through his Holy Spirit and the prayers and advice of many to mold the Marcos into a stronger family.

That God is succeeding became evident in what Jeff calls the "Goodbye Devotional" which took place in the Marco's home on Sunday evening, August 13, 2000. Jeff describes it this way: "We had dinner as a family and after the meal we watched a home video from January 1996. As we watched the video we saw a healthy, positive, normal family laughing and enjoying each other. There was tender affection expressed among all the family members, particularly between Lila and me. We realized from watching the video that the 'dysfunctionality' that we thought characterized our family over the last several years really wasn't all true. We had bought into Satan's lies and had accentuated the negative instead of focusing on the positive! It was extremely uplifting for our family to realize this.

"After dinner, we began our family devotional. I gave the boys each a sword that had been crafted for them and a plaque that stated my dreams for them. I shared exactly what each boy meant to me as a son. They each read aloud and gave to me a letter that they had each written, sharing their heartfelt love for me. (Lila told me later that Chris had written his letter with her help. He would write a word, stop, look up at her with tears in his eyes and say, 'Mommy, every time I write the words, it makes it hurt.')

"As I talked about Lila, I apologized for past mistakes, lifted her up and praised her for being there 'in sickness and in health.' I realized that sometimes we go through the motions and just say the vows without realizing that one day there may be an 'in sickness' time. I gave her a necklace as a statement of my love and gratitude.

"She shared that she greatly appreciated the 'tremendous father' that I have been and still am to the boys. She told me that she was exceedingly grateful for our marriage and that she would miss me greatly. The dinner was filled with laughter and the devotional with tears. This was a day to remember forever. We had a time as a family where we reclaimed what Satan had taken away. We cleared the slate on everything!

"There are no regrets! We all felt complete resolution, full resolution of all conflicts and hurts—past as well as any that may occur in the future."

The Impact on the Community

Jeff and Lila can share many examples of the positive impact their faithful struggle has produced within the community. According to Jeff, "It has increased our faith as a family to see God work through my life and prolong it to the amazement of the health care professionals. What was supposed to be a life span of only weeks, or at best months when I was first diagnosed, has turned into four and a half years. I've shared my faith with the physicians who have cared for me and they know that there is 'something different' keeping me alive. One of the nurses was amazed at how 'fat' my patient folder is, 'because,' she said, 'most people in your condition have thin folders.'"

Jeff wonders how Chris's schoolteacher has been affected by a paper he wrote on the first day of school. "Chris was given an assignment to write a short paper about his summer vacation and his family. He wrote: 'My mommy's a nurse. My daddy has cancer. Aaron's going to Duke. Brian is in high school.' Then he wrote, 'Sometimes I have a tough time. My daddy is dying, but he gave me a sword to remember him.'"

Growth of the Disciples

Jeff has been greatly encouraged by the church's response to his family's needs. He said, "At the onset of my illness, most of the disciples weren't sure of how to meet our family's needs. They have grown with me as my needs have grown. It is a testament to the power of the Holy Spirit to see how he has revealed to others not only how to meet our family's physical needs, but our emotional and spiritual needs as well. A recent conversation that took place between one of the church leaders and me illustrates the point. He asked me, 'What can I do for you?' I responded, 'Ask not what the kingdom can do for me, but what I can do for the kingdom. I'm a disciple till I die. You can help me by fulfilling your role in my life as an evangelist. Keep me on track: sharing my faith, repenting of sin and serving. Watch that I do not demonstrate fear in the face of death, which would be a slap in the face of God. Say to me, 'Jeff, get a grip!' Be there to help me if I should stumble. All of my physical needs are met; consider the spiritual battle going on; be an evangelist. Call me to do what I need to do!'"

Daily Renewal

Our time together slipped by so quickly. Jeff was tired and we needed to stop our discussion. He was tired and I was full. I was sitting across from a man who embodies 2 Corinthians 4:7-18! Jeff Marco had just shown me that no matter what trials we face, God has promised to be with us, to strengthen us and to mold us into his image,

> Therefore we do not lose heart. Though outwardly we are wasting away, yet inwardly we are being renewed day by day. For our light and momentary troubles are achieving for us an eternal

glory that far outweighs them all. So we fix our eyes not on what is seen, but on what is unseen. For what is seen is temporary, but what is unseen is eternal. (2 Corinthians 4:16-18)

31

Even in Prison
Nothing Can Separate Us from the Love of Christ
Ronnie Boyd

One day in the summer of 1987, I didn't have money because the night before I had spent all I had on drugs. It was about 2:30 P.M. and I needed to be at work at 4:00 P.M. As I had no money, I jumped the turnstile instead of paying for the subway. I started up the stairway, but was stopped by a plainclothes policeman who pulled me over into the corner. He then showed me his badge and stated he was an officer. During this time, two other police officers came running up the stairs. They showed their badges and reported that they were going to arrest me for a crime that had been committed one year earlier. At first, I didn't believe it. But when they put the handcuffs on me, I knew it was for real. My heart was pounding and I was anxious and afraid. I just kept telling the cops that I didn't do the crime. They told me to shut up and tell it to the judge.

Charged by Men, Forgiven by God

That night, I went to a place called Central Booking. This is where your picture and fingerprints are taken and extensive background checks are performed. I got to see the judge the following day and was asked to enter a plea—innocent or guilty. Of course I pleaded innocent, because I was then and am still completely innocent of the crime with which I was charged. The judge set bail at $1,500. The prosecutor was present and she was against my having bail at all.

She stated that the crime was a serious offense. In legal terms, I was charged with robbery and assault in the second degree. A year prior to my arrest, an eighty-two-year-old woman had been robbed of eight dollars and beaten up. An eyewitness to the crime had seen me walking to the train station at the time of my arrest and went and notified the police, who then followed me to the train station and arrested me.

I made bail (my sister posted the money) and so was able to go to work each day. Shortly after this arrest, I was invited to the New York City church by an old friend from grade school. Every Saturday for three weeks straight, I ran into this friend. Finally, in late August of 1987, I decided to attend a midweek service on 76th Street. I studied the Bible for about a month, and on September 14, 1987, I was baptized into Christ at the Beacon Theater in New York and was forgiven of all my sins. When I studied the Bible with the brothers, I made them aware of the charges that I was facing.

My next court appearance was in October of 1987. I appeared in court that month and the judge prepared me for the task of going to trial. I was given a court-appointed lawyer who kept telling me that he knew the judge who would be presiding over my trial and that I would go free. After my court date in October, the judge set another date for the second week of December. During this time, I had moved out of the Bronx and moved in with brothers living on Bleecker Street in Manhattan. I was also attending the Chemical Recovery (CR) group. (I had had one relapse on drugs in the middle of November.) During my next court appearance, my bail was revoked, which meant that until my trial date, I would need to remain in jail.

That day was a sad and scary one for me. When I got to the Bronx House of Detention, I called the brothers I was living with and told them the whole story. They asked me when my next court appearance was, and I told them that I would see the judge the following day. When I appeared in court, there in the courtroom were brothers and sisters from the church. It was an encouragement to my heart to see Christians. The night before I had not slept well at all. The bed I had slept on was hard, it was an extremely cold night, and I was surrounded by iron bars. I felt cold and isolated. I was afraid about what would happen to me, and as I stood before the judge that day, it was very clear to me that this case was going to trial. I was now faced with the decision of having a jury trial or a judge trial. Not only that, but if I decided to go with a jury and I lost the case, I would be facing a maximum of fifteen years in prison.

The Shocking Verdict

The fear and anxiety that I felt that day were unbearable. I just cried when the judge said my case was going to trial. My entire life was on the line at this point. I thought that by my becoming a Christian, God would take care of this matter. As I was being led away back to jail, the sisters in the courtroom were crying as well.

My trial date was set for the second week of January 1988. As I sat in jail during that time, I knew that I needed to make a decision about whether I still wanted to be a Christian or not. I didn't want to be a hypocrite. I'd seen too many of those both inside of prison and out and I didn't want to fake it. I was angry, afraid and hurt that this was happening to me. I felt alone and I was in a very isolated place. I thought, "How could God let this happen to me?"

So one night, I thought through my life and all I had gained through drugs, dropping out of high school, losing everything I had and now being in jail. And I thought about the decision I had made just three months earlier to serve God with all my heart, mind and soul. I prayed and read my Bible more than I ever had. I cried to God that night because it was a thin line between the world and the kingdom of God. After reading and praying, I sat on my bed and made a conscious decision that I would remain a Christian in spite of my circumstances. It was a hard choice, but the greatest choice I've ever made.

As the trial was drawing near, day after day the brothers would visit me and write me letters of encouragement. I still battled with fear at this time because I did not know how much time I would spend in prison if things didn't go well. I told my lawyer that I would waive the jury and go with the judge. I thought that going with the judge would be a smart move because he knew the law, and besides, I didn't do the crime I was charged with.

Finally, the day came when the trial was to begin. Those present at the trial included the judge, prosecutor, me and my court-appointed lawyer. Watching the trial were about thirty disciples.

This impressed the judge. The trial lasted two days. The prosecutor presented the case against me. The elderly woman who had been robbed and assaulted was there, as well as the eyewitness who claimed to have chased me on the day of the crime. Then my lawyer stated my side of the case. He allowed my evangelist and the sister who had invited me to church to testify on my behalf. They gave an account of how I had changed during the prior several months. The sister started crying on the stand because of the questions she was asked. This went on for two days. Then it was time for the judge to decide on the case.

On the day of his decision the courtroom was jammed with disciples. The judge entered the courtroom and everyone rose. He said that he had considered all the facts. He had me stand up after announcing my name. He looked at me and said that I was a Saul who had turned into a Paul and that he was impressed with the level of support that I had received from the church. He also said that he hoped they would stick by me to the end, and when he said that, my heart started pounding. Then came the bombshell: the judge said that, after careful review of the facts, he had found me guilty as charged. All I could hear at that time were people in the background crying and some who were in disbelief. I just stood in handcuffs crying as the verdict was read.

Two weeks later, I appeared before the judge for sentencing as well as for my chance to speak about the charges against me. During this time, the church had written letters to the judge, asking for leniency on my behalf. The judge stated that he had received the letters of support and had considered all that was written. He asked me if I wanted to say anything concerning the case, and I said yes. All that I could think in my mind was the verse that says that the Lord detests both acquitting the guilty and condemning the innocent, but what came out of my mouth was something different. I proclaimed my innocence and invited the judge to church, and that was all. Then the judge sentenced me to the least amount of time in jail, one-and-a-half to four-and-a-half years.

Drawing Near to God

Prison is a very frightening place to be. There are drugs, fighting and sex, which take place on a daily basis. All these events

I was exposed to, but never participated in. I witnessed many horrible events and decided to draw closer to God daily to protect me from the evil I witnessed. So for the next two years I studied my Bible daily, drew closer to God, and received and wrote many letters to the church in Manhattan. Many Christians came to visit me while I was in prison. The support I received from the church was strong and helped keep me faithful to God. While in prison, I studied the Bible with many people and started a Bible talk on Monday nights.

I decided that God had allowed this to happen to me to draw me closer to him—it was his plan to keep me faithful. It was hard for me during this time, but I made every effort to stay close to Jesus. Some of my favorite stories in the Bible were those about Joseph, Paul, Peter, and even Jeremiah, all of whom were in jail, but walked closely with God.

On July 19, 1989, I walked out of prison a free man. There are no words to explain the relief and joy I felt. I had forty dollars and a bus ticket to Port Authority Bus Terminal in Manhattan. When I arrived at the bus terminal, there stood a number of Christians to greet me. The first thing I did was go to a restaurant and order steak and French fries. It was a feast and celebration. Upon arriving at my apartment, I was greeted by a surprise party, with Christians I had met before and some I didn't know. I was home after nearly two years, back with disciples and ready to continue serving in God's kingdom.

What I learned in prison has spiritually carried me through in my walk with God. I've led Bible talks, house churches, campus ministries and CR ministries since I've been a Christian. Today I'm fourteen years old as a disciple, married, with two wonderful children, ages four and two. I've returned to school and earned a degree. I am currently enrolled at a master's program at New York University. Recently, God blessed me with an appointment as a deacon in the East Side region of the New York church.

When I first became a Christian, I was a high-school dropout with very limited education and people skills. My jail experience was God's saving grace in my life. God was molding and shaping me to remain faithful to him no matter what. I wouldn't wish prison on anyone I know because of the horror of living in such circumstances. On the other hand, for a Christian in these circumstances, it can build your character for God, allow you to become spiritually strong, and totally test your faith, love and commitment to him. No matter what your own situation, remember the Lord and stay close to him.

This story originally appeared on the Web site for the International Churches of Christ (www.icoc.org) and is used here by permission.

Contributors

- **Jim Blough** is the world sector administrator for the churches in the Commonwealth World Sector of the International Churches of Christ and an elder in the Washington D.C. church.
- **Ronnie Boyd** is a non-staff leader in the New York City Church of Christ.
- **Jim Brown** is an evangelist in the New York City Church of Christ.
- **Doug Cameron** is a region elder in the Boston Church of Christ and a leader in the spiritual recovery ministry.
- **Jeff Chacon** is an evangelist with the San Diego Church of Christ.
- **Jeff Chappell** is an evangelist in the Boston Church of Christ.
- **Jaime De Anda, Ph.D.,** is the world sector administrator for the churches in the Central and South America World Sector of the International Churches of Christ.
- **Gordon Ferguson** is an elder, evangelist and teacher with the Boston Church of Christ. He is the author of nine books.
- **Mike Fontenot** is the lead evangelist for the church in Norfolk, Virginia, and the co-author of *The Prideful Soul's Guide to Humility.*
- **Jack Frederick** is a senior development engineer with the a major defense contractor and a regional elder in the Boston Church of Christ.
- **Andrew Giambarba** is the lead evangelist for the South Florida Church of Christ and a geographic sector leader in the Central and South America World Sector of the International Churches of Christ.
- **Mike Hammonds** is a non-staff leader in the Boston Church of Christ and a financial planner.
- **Ryan Howard** is a disciple in the San Diego Church of Christ and is licensed in the state of California as a marriage, family and child counselor.
- **Steve Johnson** is the lead evangelist for the New York City Church of Christ and the world sector leader for the ACES World Sector of the International Churches of Christ.
- **Thomas Jones** is senior editor for Discipleship Publications and a region elder in the Boston church. He is the author of four books.
- **Declan Joyce** is a disciple in the New York City Church of Christ and the editorial director for the Kingdom News Network.
- **Tom Kuhn** is an elder for the South Florida Church of Christ and works as a senior design analyst with a leading producer of banking and financial software.

- **Sam Laing** is the lead evangelist for the Triangle church in North Carolina, the author of five books, and a teacher in the ACES World Sector of the International Churches of Christ.
- **Tracy Larr** is an evangelist and regional elder in the Boston Church of Christ.
- **Rick Luz** is an administrator for the Boston Church of Christ.
- **Steve Major** is disciple in the Boston Church of Christ who owns his own Web development company.
- **Kevin McDaniel** is an evangelist with the Boston Church of Christ.
- **Randy McKean** is the lead evangelist for the Boston Church of Christ and the world sector leader for the New England and Europe World Sector of the International Churches of Christ.
- **Michael Newman** is a disciple in the Los Angeles Church of Christ and a marriage and family therapist intern, working to be licensed by the state of California at the end of his internship.
- **Kelly Petre** is the editor-in-chief of Discipleship Publications International and an evangelist in the Boston Church of Christ.
- **Mark Schnell** is a quality assurance manager with a manufacturing company and a non-staff leader in the Boston Church of Christ.
- **Mark Shaw** is a non-staff leader in the Berlin Church of Christ.
- **Wyndham Shaw** is an elder and evangelist in the Boston Church of Christ and a vice-president with HOPE Worldwide.
- **Mike Taliaferro** is the lead evangelist for the church in Johannesburg, South Africa, the author of three books, and the leader of the International Churches of Christ in Africa.
- **Ben Weast** and his wife, Beth, lead the children's ministry for the Triangle Church of Christ in Durham, North Carolina.

Who Are We?

Discipleship Publications International (DPI) began publishing in 1993. We are a nonprofit Christian publisher affiliated with the International Churches of Christ, committed to publishing and distributing materials that honor God, lift up Jesus Christ and show how his message practically applies to all areas of life. We have a deep conviction that no one changes life like Jesus and that the implementation of his teaching will revolutionize any life, any marriage, any family and any singles household.

Since our beginning, we have published more than 110 titles; plus, we have produced a number of important, spiritual audio products. More than one million volumes have been printed, and our works have been translated into more than a dozen languages—international is not just a part of our name! Our books are shipped regularly to every inhabited continent.

To see a more detailed description of our works, find us on the World Wide Web at www.dpibooks.org. You can order books by calling 1-888-DPI-BOOK twenty-four hours a day. From outside the U.S., call 978-670-8840 ext. 227 during Boston-area business hours.

We appreciate the hundreds of comments we have received from readers. We would love to hear from you. Here are other ways to get in touch:

Mail: DPI, 2 Sterling Road, Billerica, Mass. 01862-2595
E-Mail: dpibooks@icoc.org

Find Us on the
World Wide Web

www.dpibooks.org

1-888-DPI-BOOK

outside the U.S.,
call 978-670-8840 ext. 227